THE SPIRITUAL BASIS OF REAL PROSPERITY

Books by the Author

The Path of Light
The Self-Revealed Knowledge
That Liberates the Spirit
Living in God
The Book of Life
An Easy Guide to Ayurveda
An Easy Guide to Meditation
A Master Guide to Meditation
Life Surrendered in God
(Patanjali's yoga-sutras)

The Eternal Way
(The Inner Meaning of
the Bhagavad Gita)

THE
SPIRITUAL
BASIS OF REAL
PROSPERITY

How to Always Be in the Flow
of Resources and Supportive
Events and Relationships
for Your Highest Good

ROY EUGENE DAVIS

CSA Press · Lakemont, Georgia 30552-0007

CSA Press • Post Office Box 7
Lakemont, Georgia 30552-0007 (U.S.A.)
Offices on Lake Rabun Road

Telephone (706) 782-4723   Fax (706) 782-4560
E-mail csainc@stc.net   www.csa-davis.org

CSA Press is the publishing department
of Center for Spiritual Awareness.

This book is available in West Africa from:
Centre For Spiritual Awareness, P.O. Box 507, Accra, Ghana.

Printed and Manufactured in the United States of America

Our birth is but a sleep and a forgetting:
The soul that rises with us, our life's star,
 Hath had elsewhere it setting,
  And cometh from afar.
 Not in entire forgetfulness,
 And not in utter nakedness,
But trailing clouds of glory do we come
 From God, who is our home:

*William Wordsworth / Ode. Intimations of Immortality
from Recollections of Early Childhood*

INTRODUCTION

In the following pages I do not offer any formulas for getting rich quickly or for discovering immediate solutions to all personal problems. What *is* explained are reliable, tested and verified ways to experience satisfying spiritual growth and live happily and effectively. My thesis is simple: for prosperity to be real or authentic, it must be based on an awareness of spiritual realities and on compliant cooperation with the principles which enable it to be experienced. That this information needs to be widely published is obvious to anyone who is observant.

In 1994, a department of the United Nations published a progress report to provide information about global conditions and human affairs. It reported that, in comparison to conditions fifty years previously, more people had access to food and literacy levels were higher. Even so, almost two billion people, most of them in economically undeveloped regions of the world, were impoverished. Approximately one third of the planet's human inhabitants were illiterate. The gap between rich people and poor people had widened. In some countries, the average annual income per person was less than three hundred dollars. Ten countries had nearly seventy percent of the world's poorest people.

Other sources report that global human population is increasing at the rate of eighty million people every year: approximately six and a half million a month; one and a half million each week; more than two hundred thousand each day. According to a report published by World Watch Institute, there are already some signs of faltering growth trends in countries that were expected to have the greatest population increases in the near future. Population in thirty-two industrialized countries has stabilized because of declining birthrates.

A few countries, including Russia, Italy, the United States, and Japan, have declining populations. In some developing countries where population growth will probably be slower in a few years, more people are dying. India, Pakistan, and Nigeria, for instance, are beginning to experience difficulty in feeding, housing, and educating increasing numbers of children while having to confront the challenges of falling water tables, deforestation, and soil erosion caused in part by rapid population growth in recent decades. Some observers of global trends are of the opinion that human population growth will slow down because developing countries will begin to encourage smaller families or unrestrained birth rates will result in the spread of famine and disease. The major threats to human security on the planet are conflicts within nations because of socioeconomic deprivation and differences, and ethnic and religious intolerance.

In the United States, it is estimated that one percent of the population (approximately 2.8 million people) own forty percent of the wealth; ten percent (approximately 28 million) own ninety percent; ninety percent (252 million) own ten percent. Fifty percent of the people who work for wages in the United States do not have enough money saved to pay their bills if they were unable to work for six months. Fewer than ten percent have enough money saved to meet their personal needs when they are no longer able to work or choose to retire. Most older Americans, although they have a place to live and may have a modest income from a pension plan or from investments, are also financially dependent on social security checks or assistance provided by family members. By the year 2015, over sixty percent of the population of the United States and several countries in Europe will be over sixty-five years of age, and will live many more years.

Because of the rapid increase of knowledge and technological breakthroughs, conditions on the planet have changed more dramatically in the past two hundred years than during the previous ten thousand years. In the nineteenth century, railroads and access to electricity made a notable impact on people's lives. In the 20th century, radio, the telephone, automobiles, air transportation, computers, scientific advancement, and space exploration broadened our view of the universe and enabled us to ponder near and distant future possibilities yet to be discovered and actualized.

Concurrent with the many changes that have been rapidly occurring, there has been a noticeable surge of sincere interest in spirituality and in discovering and focusing on life's real values. Many more people are endeavoring to learn how to enjoy healthy, long life which has both depth and meaning. Many are also actively seeking a means by which they may facilitate their spiritual growth, comprehend the reality of God, have accurate knowledge about their relationship to the universe, and be assured of their future well-being after their relatively brief sojourn in this space-time realm is concluded.

The information in this book will be of value to the reader who aspires to total well-being and is willing to be responsible for actualizing and maintaining it. I recommend that it first be read in its entirety, then the text perused until the ideas and principles are clearly understood. In a notebook or private journal, write your specific plans to implement constructive actions and immediately actualize your plans with unwavering, self-disciplined resolve.

Acquired knowledge that is not applied is merely information; right application of useful knowledge will produce gratifying results. Be curious and enthusiastic. You are in this world to learn, grow, be expressive, prosper in all ways, and fulfill your spiritual destiny.

May all of your worthy aspirations be fulfilled and may all of your meaningful purposes be accomplished.

ROY EUGENE DAVIS

Lakemont, Georgia
January, 1999

CONTENTS

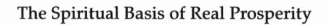

The Spiritual Basis of Real Prosperity

CHAPTER ONE

The Spiritual Basis of Real Prosperity

Life need not be difficult, painful, or restricted. Anyone who is capable of rational thinking can choose to be spiritually awake and serenely happy, live effectively, have life-enhancing desires fulfilled, and consistently accomplish meaningful purposes.

To fully actualize life's highest potential, we have only to aspire to excellence, be decisive, have or acquire knowledge that enables us to act wisely and skillfully, persist with firm resolve, and willingly and appropriately participate with the laws of causation that can produce the desired results.

The spiritual basis of real prosperity is alert awareness of our wholeness as spiritual beings that provides a clear perception of the universe as an undivided or whole manifestation of cosmic forces emanating from and sustained by a field of Infinite Consciousness. If we are not always able to thus perceive ourselves and the universe— or if restrictive circumstances are common or occasionally occur and persist—clarification of our awareness that restores it to wholeness is needed.

The words *prosper* and *prosperity* are derived from the Latin word *prosperus*: fortunate. To *prosper* is to thrive, flourish, and be successful; to be affluent: in a continuous flow of resources and supportive events and relationships which assure our highest good. Prosperity is experienced when the spiritual, mental, physical, and environmental components of life are harmoniously integrated.

We are truly prosperous when we:

• Are spiritually aware.
• Are mentally, emotionally, and physically healthy.
• Have harmonious, mutually satisfying relationships with people with whom we associate.
• Can appropriately relate to the world and its ongoing events and circumstances with confidence.
• Can efficiently perform our duties and consistently accomplish our meaningful purposes.
• Have our life-enhancing desires easily fulfilled.
• Always have resources available that provide for our well-being and enable us to live effectively.

The one field of Consciousness which manifests the energies and forms of Nature is self-referring. Because it alone exists, it interacts only with itself. Everything in the realm of objective Nature—light, the quantum field, atoms, molecules, electricity, magnetism, various forms of matter, living things, and the minds and bodies of creatures and human beings—are aspects of the creative power of Consciousness produced by its interactions.

Since all souls that animate bodies are expressive aspects of Consciousness, and Nature is composed of its emanated forces, why do creatures and human beings suffer misfortune and experience hardship and deprivation? Cells, microbes, viruses, bacteria, aquatic life, insects, birds, and animals instinctively thrive when conditions are ideal for their needs. They endeavor to adapt to conditions which threaten their survival and are deprived or die when environmental circumstances are not supportive of them. Human beings, similarly survival-oriented and with intelligence, instincts, and acquired adaptive behaviors, also require supportive environmental circumstances if they are to thrive, satisfy their urges, and fulfill their purposes.

Human beings are (usually) more conscious than simpler forms of life. Our refined brain and nervous system enable us to have the potential to be more conscious, more intelligent, imaginative, choose our behaviors, and have a considerable degree of control over our environment and circumstances. Although our self-determined behaviors can sometimes get us into trouble, when they are wisely chosen they can be the means by which we may create or choose ideal circumstances for ourselves and others.

Having an abundance of material things is not of itself evidence of real prosperity. We may have a surplus of material things and other resources yet be spiritually impoverished, have poor physical health, be psychologically disturbed, or be severely challenged by a variety of problems and difficulties. We may be healthy and enjoy comfortable relationships, yet be unable or unwilling to effectively relate to the material world or have an adequate supply of its resources. Symptoms of lack of spiritual awareness—neurosis, psychosis, poor health, addictive behaviors, mental confusion, emotional unrest and immaturity, and thoughts and feelings of insecurity, loneliness, and despair—may be experienced by people who are financially secure and those who are not.

When we direct our attention to the subject of money, questions may arise in the mind. Why are many honest, sincerely spiritually inclined people unable to be successful in their endeavors or to demonstrate overall prosperity in their lives? Why are some people, who are not spiritually awake, whose behaviors are quite ordinary (or neurotic or dysfunctional), wealthy?

Whatever is possible to be experienced by people who are egocentric (self-conscious) can and may occur because their awareness is dreamlike; they are only partially conscious. Incidents of misfortune or of good fortune are not always directly related to their superficial thoughts or random actions.

Habitual states of consciousness primarily determine personal circumstances, prevailing over even heroic endeavors to think constructively or to act effectively. Some people who do not know about metaphysical principles of causation may have well-developed powers of concentration, be strongly motivated, and have skills which enable them to accomplish their purposes. Others, with knowledge of how to function effectively may not fervently desire to do so, or may be inhibited by psychological or other problems.

With even a modest degree of spiritual awareness and knowledge of the principles of cause and effect, we can soon learn how to determine our circumstances by our wise choices and constructive actions.

How can individuals in oppressive political, social, and economic conditions be prosperous? The principles of cause and effect that determine circumstances are impersonal and universal—they operate for anyone, anywhere, anytime. Even when conditions are oppressive, when one becomes aware that choices can be made, and makes them, constructive adjustments of states of consciousness and mental states—reinforced by constructive actions when necessary—will always result in improved circumstances.

In recent years, countless numbers of books have been published in which the authors have extolled the idea of abundance—"The universe is a manifestation of God's creative power and you can have as much of its resources as you want if you will learn how be in harmonious relationship with it." While it is true that the universe can provide for all of our needs, it is not spiritually useful to cultivate an arrogant attitude of acquisitiveness characterized by aggression, greed, and compulsive endeavors to grasp, possess, and control. It is more beneficial, and soul-satisfying, to determine what our major purposes in life are, and learn how to be sufficiently prosperous in every way so that they can be successfully accomplished.

Very few readers of books with prosperity themes experience long-term benefits. The causes vary. They may not be able to comprehend the message. They may be unable to change their point of view from conditioned, personality-centered self-conscious states to awareness of themselves as Self- (soul) determined spiritual beings. They may be easily distracted from their goals. Or, they may be complacently satisfied with their prevailing mental attitudes and thought processes, addictive behaviors, familiar circumstances, and acquired relationships.

We have a prosperity consciousness when we are undeniably aware of wholeness, of *having*. Endeavors to manifest the effects of a prosperity consciousness—mental, emotional, and physical health, intellectual discernment, creativity, orderly circumstances, supportive relationships, timely events, and abundant resources—without vivid awareness of the wholeness of life will always either fall short of the goal or fail to produce permanent results. Why is this so? Because we cannot experience or manifest that which is not already in our consciousness.

When awareness of wholeness, of *having*, is our normal state, its effects are naturally expressive. States of consciousness and mental states produce effects after their own kind in accord with the natural, therefore reliable and predictable, principles of causation. Our personal experiences, behaviors, and circumstances always perfectly correspond with our habitual, subjective states of consciousness, mental attitudes, dominant thoughts, and consciously known or subliminal desires.

Because states of consciousness and mental states can cause effects, every person—happy or unhappy, healthy or unhealthy, successful or not, rich or poor—is always consciously or unconsciously flawlessly self-determining their experiences and circumstances.

A healthy-minded, emotionally mature person who desires improved circumstances will respond favorably to opportunities to learn how to be self-reliant and to live more effectively. Some individuals, whose actions have been unproductive of desired results or who prefer to believe themselves to be victims of fate, karma, adverse planetary influences, genetic factors, economic or societal trends and circumstances, or the malicious thoughts or actions of others, may not want to be reminded that they are contributing to their suffering and misfortune. They may complain, asserting that God does not love them ... life isn't fair ... others are more fortunate ... no one understands or cares about them ... they are incapable of helping themselves because they are victims of circumstances beyond their control. The truth, when apprehended, is liberating: every person who is capable of making choices can learn to be responsible for what they think, do, and experience. They can be fulfilled by acknowledging their spiritual potential and by doing what is necessary to actualize it.

If we are not spiritually aware when we endeavor to demonstrate or experience evidence of prosperity, we may be inclined to be manipulative or to nurture superstitious ideas. Inclinations to be manipulative, to control others or events or circumstances for self-centered purposes, indicate a deficiency of awareness of wholeness. Superstitious ideas, and behaviors prompted by them, indicate incomplete understanding of the nature of consciousness, mind, and the laws of cause and effect. We cannot have what we need or desire when we believe and feel that we do not already have it in our consciousness. This principle is stated in the New Testament (*Mark* 4:25):

> To one who has [a prosperity consciousness], more shall be given: from one who does not have it, even what little he has will be taken away from him.

Whatever we claim or possess in our consciousness is ours in fact. That which we do not, cannot, or will not claim in our consciousness is not substantial.

No one, and nothing outside of us, can take from us what is established in our consciousness. No one, and nothing outside of us, can permanently provide for us what is not already established in our consciousness. When wholeness is realized (clearly known and vividly experienced), it pervades our consciousness, mind, body, and environment. When beliefs and illusions of lack or limitation are forever banished from our mind and awareness, we cannot experience lack, nor can obstacles to personal expression, creative endeavor, or successful accomplishment of purposes prevail.

If it seems that our resources, including money, are inadequate to meet our needs or to enable us to easily do the things we need—or want—to do, the problem is not a deficiency of resources. Deficiency in a whole, self-complete universe is impossible. The problem can only be that we have yet to be spiritually aware; effectively use our time, energy, and talents; and wisely manage the resources we have.

How do you live your life?

- Are your activities well-ordered?
- Do you have priorities: duties, routines, or actions that you perform first because they are essential to your well-being and to living effectively and accomplishing your purposes?
- Do you think that you do not have enough time to do what you want to do or to accomplish what needs to be done?
- Do you perform nonproductive actions merely to appear to be busy, to avoid boredom, or to avoid having to think about more important matters?
- Have you eliminated nonessential, nonproductive actions?
- Have you renounced personal relationships and social activities that are meaningless or which distract your attention?
- Do you pray and meditate on a regular schedule?
- Do you plan your work and other important activities so that you can efficiently accomplish your purposes, or

are you drifting without a sense of meaningful purpose?
• Do you allow behaviors, personal relationships, and circumstances to be determined by your moods and whims while naively thinking that the Spirit of God or your inner guidance is directing your path in life?

We *can* have guidance: the spiritual impulses that determine our destiny can be influential and our intuition can provide insight. However, if our sense of guidance is erroneous or if constructive, life-enhancing events and circumstances are not unfolding, we need to more carefully examine the thoughts and feelings we have presumed to be indications of guidance. We need to be practical and to skillfully use our common sense.

Are you:

• Energetic, enthusiastic, and glad to be alive?
• Do you enjoy living?
• Are you goal-oriented?
• Are you sincerely committed to awakening to your full spiritual potential as soon as possible?
• Do you have an abundance of energy?
• Are you using your energy wisely?

Vital forces are weakened and wasted by:

• Superficial, useless talking.
• Unhealthy dietary habits.
• Irregular lifestyle routines.
• Addictive behaviors.
• Restlessness.
• Purposeless actions.

- Excessive stimulation of the senses.
- Insufficient sleep.
- Obsessive or habitual daydreaming or fantasy.
- Worry.
- Neglect of stress management routines.

Although we receive energy from the food we eat and the air we breathe, the body's primary energy source is soul force. The vital force that enlivens and nourishes the body is increased and transformed into finer, regenerative energies by:

- Constructive thinking.
- Enthusiastic, intentional living to successfully accomplish meaningful purposes.
- Optimism: being habitually inclined to expect the best possible outcomes from personal endeavors and to emphasize the most positive aspects of a situation.
- Prayer, and meditation that clarifies awareness.
- Wholesome lifestyle routines that include a balance of purposeful activity with sufficient rest, relaxation, recreational activities, stress management routines, and nutritious foods that are easily assimilated.
- Having a keen interest in living, learning, growing to mental and emotional maturity, relating knowledgeably and effectively to the universe, accomplishing worthwhile purposes, unfolding innate potential, and fulfilling spiritual destiny to be Self-realized and God-conscious.

How skillfully do you use your talents and abilities?

- Do you know that your potential to unfold and to live effectively is limitless?

- Are your desires constructive and life-enhancing?
- Are you honest, compassionate, and caring?
- Are you fully aware of your talents and abilities?
- Have you developed and are you using your talents and abilities to their full extent?
- Are you willing to learn how to live more effectively?
- Can you easily comprehend the meaning of what you see, read, or hear? If not, are you willing to improve your powers of perception and your reading and comprehension skills?
- Are you self-motivated to perform actions that are entirely constructive?
- Do you have a clear sense of purpose for your life? If you do, act now to fulfill it. If you do not, ponder the matter until you discover it, then resolve to fulfill it.
- Do you have habits of thinking, feeling, or behavior that restrict your ability to live effectively? If so, replace them with constructive actions.
- Are you aware of circumstances that are restrictive or impose limits? If so decide to improve, heal, or change them, and do so.
- Do you enjoy using your intellectual abilities?
- Can you easily use your intuitive powers?
- Are you a possibility-thinker? Are you able to think of and mentally envision ideal solutions to problems, alternative conditions to replace those which are unsatisfying, the final results of your constructive endeavors, and supportive circumstances and relationships for your highest good and the highest good of others? Is possibility-thinking habitual, or do you do it only when challenged or in need?
- Do you habitually exercise pure intention to cause

desired outcomes of endeavors to occur or to attract supportive events and circumstances into your life?

Whether your lifestyle is simple and your needs are few, or your lifestyle is expansive and more resources are needed to accomplish your purposes—whatever is needed the universe can easily supply. The universe is whole and self-sufficient. Its energy and substance is constant: energy manifests as material things and material things are transformed into energy.

If we lack spiritual awareness, peace of mind, health, knowledge, skills, opportunities, supportive relationships, resources—anything that we need to enable us to live effectively—we have only to replace our illusions of limitation with accurate perceptions of the wholeness of life and of possibilities for fulfillment, then live in accord with our higher understanding.

Guidelines for Self-Evaluation and Purposeful Planning

To experience optimal (most favorable) benefits, obtain a notebook in which to write your insights, needs, goals, and specific plans to accomplish your meaningful purposes. Doing this will clarify your thinking and enable you to live effectively. As you write, remember that you are a spiritual being—superior to mental, emotional, and physical states and mundane circumstances. Keep your notebook in a private place. To help you to maintain the momentum of your progress, refer to what you have written from time to time. Make new notations to refresh your resolve or record your success in accomplishing your purposes. Feel prosperous. Think and act decisively.

1.   Review the chapter and write your responses to the questions asked in the text.

2.   If you have opinions, feelings, mental attitudes, or habitual behaviors that need to be changed to allow you to live more effectively, write what you need to do and be firmly committed to doing it.

3.   Write your needs, goals, projects, and specific plans to perform any necessary actions.

There is a fundamental purpose for our lives. To know it, we must understand where life comes from and where it is going. We must consider life's highest potential for development and look beyond our immediate goals to what we ultimately want to accomplish.

— *Paramahansa Yogananda*

When you understand the truth of suffering, its cause, its remedy, and the means of its cessation, the four noble truths will be comprehended. You will walk the right path. Right views will be the torch that lights your way. Right aspirations will be your guide. Right speech will be your dwelling place on life's road. Your way will be straight, for it is right behavior. Your nourishment will be the right means of earning your livelihood. Right endeavors will be your steps. Right thoughts will be your breath. Right contemplation will provide abiding peace.

— *Teachings of Gautama, the Buddha*

_____

CHAPTER TWO

Prosperity is a Personal Choice

If life need not be difficult, painful, or restricted, why do many people continue to experience hardship, suffering, and limitation? Some causes may be:

- Lack of knowledge of how to live effectively.
- Inability to perform effective actions because of lack of experience.
- Resistance to learning.
- Reluctance to modify mental attitudes, emotional states, and personal behaviors.
- Reluctance to grow to emotional maturity.
- Lack of desire to live effectively.

Knowledge can be acquired and applied. Skills can be learned, improved, and perfected. Resistance to learning, reluctance to modify mental and emotional states and grow to emotional maturity, and lack of desire to live effectively may be reinforced by:

- Absence of a clear sense of meaningful purpose.
- Fear of change.
- Attachment to existing circumstances.
- Apathy: indifference, passivity.
- Egotism: arrogance, an exaggerated and unrealistic sense of self-importance, knowledge, and ability.

• Mental perversity: self-centered willfulness which may incline one to be obstinate: to habitually oppose constructive ideas or to persist in destructive or nonuseful behaviors.

• Acquiescence to the acquired habits of provincialism and mediocrity.

A life lived without meaningful purpose is wasted. That which is meaningful to us is of value, of real benefit. What we think, feel, or do that enhances our lives and benefits others and the environment is meaningful. Thoughts, moods, and actions which diminish our lives or which do not benefit others or the environment are meaningless.

To prosper and fulfill your soul destiny:

• Engage only in constructive endeavors. In accord with what you are best qualified to do because of your knowledge and skills, and what your duties are, do everything cheerfully and skillfully. Your actions will then always be entirely constructive and supportive of others and of evolutionary trends. Your mind will be peaceful. The processes of Nature will always be fully supportive of you.

• Learn to have the desires which support and enhance your life easily fulfilled. Whenever an impulse to do something worthwhile or to have a life-enhancing experience arises, or a need is present, desires naturally surface in the mind along with an urge to have them fulfilled. Use your powers of intellectual and intuitive discernment. Learn to recognize the difference between desires which support and enhance your life and desires which are unnecessary or which, if allowed to be compelling, will dis-

turb your peace of mind or contribute to other problems.
• Learn to let the universe satisfy your needs. The universe is whole; nothing is lacking. Whatever is needed for your well-being, for desires to be fulfilled or for meaningful purposes to be accomplished, is either already available, can be attracted if necessary, or can be manifested by the universe.
• Adhere to practices that will facilitate your spiritual growth. The innate urge of your Being is to be Self- and God-realized—to know and experience the truth of your Being and the wholeness of Consciousness. Until your awareness is fully restored to wholeness and you are living effectively, the possibilities for experiencing pain, difficulty, and restriction will continue to exist.

Choose to be prosperous: to be spiritually aware, healthy-minded, emotionally mature, physically vital, functionally effective, and in a continuous flow of resources and supportive events and circumstances. This is not a selfish choice. We cannot successfully assist others to discover and actualize their potential if we are not knowledgeable, fulfilled, and functional.

Fear of change can most easily be removed by nurturing an attitude of healthy-minded curiosity and by experimenting with procedures which will definitely provide experiences that are wholesome and satisfying.

Our circumstances are the evidential effects of our past and present actions; we did something to cause or to allow them to manifest. We performed an action, had a desire, formed an intention, thought of an event or circumstance as a possibility to be experienced, or consciously or unconsciously agreed to accept the opinions of others or the results of their actions. If unwanted circumstances are prevailing, we are choosing to allow them to persist. If we sincerely desire to improve or replace them, we can do so by choice, intention, and appropriate actions.

The primary cause of illness, neurosis, discord, loneliness, confusion, suffering, misfortune, poverty, and all other restrictive or unpleasant conditions, is insufficient knowledge and awareness of ourselves as spiritual beings because of mistaken self-identity; a condition described as egoism.

When we are not aware of our true nature, we tend to identify our awareness with habitual mental processes, emotional states, personality characteristics, physical conditions, and environmental circumstances and influences. Soul awareness is then somewhat confined, blurred, and fragmented. Delusions (erroneous ideas and beliefs) and illusions (the results of inaccurate perceptions) prevail. Instinctual drives and subconscious conditionings overly influence and determine decisions, actions, and reactions. Even so, we may occasionally have intuitive intimations of the reality of our true nature that are reassuring and glimpses of possibilities which are available to us that temporarily elicit a surge of inspiration, provide us hope, and impel us to our destined, higher good.

Attachments to circumstances may be due to habit; inclinations to conform to the expectations or behaviors of others; a false sense of security (believing or feeling that what presently exists is more reliable than what may or may not unfold in the near or distant future); a desire to hold on to a situation so that one's life may have the appearance of stability; or complacency. Attachments to relationships and things may be due to sentiment nurtured by lack of discernment, feelings of insecurity, loneliness, or avarice (excessive desire to possess: greed). Tenacious attachment to opinions, viewpoints, moods, sensations, behaviors, material things, situations, circumstances, or relationships are addictions. Addictions, even if not physically harmful, dissipate vital forces, weaken mental powers, inhibit emotional growth and psychological transformation, nurture neurotic tendencies, interfere with endeavors to accomplish purposes, and confine awareness.

Attachments can be renounced by:

• Analyzing why an object of desire, relationship, or experience is considered to be attractive or important and choosing to renounce them.
• Allowing emotional growth to occur.
• Spiritual practices that clarify awareness and result in intellectual and intuitive discernment.

Apathy prevails when awareness is dominated by inertia: emotional heaviness, disinterest, and mental dullness which inclines one to resist beneficial changes of circumstances, to procrastinate, or be lazy (reluctant to engage in constructive actions). Physiological causes, such as poor health, tiredness, or imbalance of the basic mind-body constitution may be contributing factors, as may mental depression or emotional exhaustion. Boredom, disinterest in or fear of exploring new possibilities, confusion, memories of past failures or rejections, or fear of future failure or rejection may be influential. Apathy can be overcome by:

• Nurturing physiological and psychological health.

• Assuming a point of view that allows possibilities to be clearly perceived or envisioned.

• Thoughtfully planning and engaging in constructive actions which will arouse innate spiritual forces, energize the body and mind, and provide a variety of opportunities for life-enhancing endeavors to be successfully accomplished.

Arrogance can be replaced by self-honest analysis of the facts regarding one's true nature. We are not the mind we use, the personality through which we present ourselves to the world, or the body through which we express. We are spiritual beings only temporarily relating to the human condition. We all have the same essence and the same capacities and qualities because we are individualized aspects of one Consciousness. When this knowledge is acquired, or spontaneously emerges from the innermost recesses of Being, arrogance is replaced by humility.

Mental perversity is a characteristic of people who are self-centered and fearful. They may be insecure, self-righteous, judgmental, opinionated, and motivated by a need to always be right or to be in control of situations. Thoughts and feelings of shame, guilt, self-disgust, and unworthiness may haunt their waking hours, disturb their sleep, and prevent them from experiencing the peace they really yearn to have. Their thoughts, desires, and behaviors may be obsessive. They may allow memories of failure, rejection, misuse or abuse by others, or their own errors of choices or behaviors to reinforce their thoughts and feelings of inferiority or lack of self-worth. Because they distrust themselves, it is often difficult for them to trust God, others, or the processes of Nature. The debilitating habit of mental perversity can be overcome by:

- Acknowledging the need to overcome the problem.
- Remembrance of one's true nature and living from that state of Being.
- Acquiring knowledge of how to live effectively and using it.
- Attitude adjustment and behavior modification.
- Emulating the behaviors of role models who are spiritually aware, healthy-minded, and prosperous.

Some common obstacles to being prosperous are:

- Lack of self-discipline.
- Irrational (confused, illusional) thinking.
- Allowing thoughts and behaviors to be determined by moods, whims, impulses generated by habits and subconscious conditionings, or the irrational opinions or behaviors of others.
- Inability or reluctance to be organized: to clearly define goals and meaningful purposes; make decisions; establish priorities (determine the difference between what is important or essential and what is not and focus attention only on important matters); and effectively use knowledge, energy, resources, skills, and abilities.
- Reluctance to relate to and learn how to effectively function in the universe which is manifesting as time, space, and matter. Some contributing factors may be lack of knowledge of how to do so; fear; emotional immaturity; or the false belief that it is wrong to want to be happy, prosperous, and fulfilled in this world—that such desires or inclinations will interfere with spiritual growth.

Thoughts or feelings that incline us to withdraw from, avoid, or resist opportunities to be happy and fulfilled should be analyzed and their causes discovered so that we know why we:

• Are averse to accepting opportunities, situations, or relationships which can be supportive of us.
• Avoid the good fortune we desire.
• Resist helpful advice.
• Allow psychological conflicts and erratic behaviors to interfere with prosperous living.
• Make excuses for not acquiring knowledge or for not adhering to lifestyle routines that nurture health and well-being.
• Procrastinate, or justify self-limiting behaviors.
• Say that we are too busy to pray and meditate.
• Say that nothing we try to accomplish works out the way we hope it will; always have bad luck; or can't help ourselves because what someone once said to us still influences our thinking or what someone did (or circumstances) caused our psychological conflicts which we are not able to remove.
• Tenaciously cling to erroneous beliefs or opinions.
• Prefer limitation, frustration, or suffering over affluence, accomplishment, and happiness.
• Allow habits, addictions, and unwise behaviors to interfere with our endeavors or our relationships when we know that we have both the freedom and the ability to renounce them.

It is our spiritual duty to be prosperous. Many people

who consider themselves to be sincere devotees of God are extremely ignorant of the basic principles of Consciousness and its processes, complacent, confused, neurotic, and dysfunctional. They mistakenly presume pleasant moods, pious thoughts, sentimental behaviors, or a naive (simplistic, devoid of analytical insight) outlook on life to be evidence of authentic spirituality. They often err by believing or proclaiming that their restrictive circumstances are caused by karmic influences or by prevailing social, cultural, or economic factors—all of which are beyond their power to control or overcome—or must be God's will for them. Only a little honest analysis would enable them to see that their experiences are directly related to their states of consciousness, thoughts, moods, and actions.

The master key to prosperous living is to first be firmly established in clear awareness of Being (our true nature), and to think and live from that state of Being. When we are spiritually awake and aware of our relationship to the totality of life:

- Our perceptions are more accurate.
- Intellectual and intuitive powers are enhanced.
- Thoughts are well-ordered and rational.
- Emotions are tranquil and appropriate.
- Right choices are more easily made.
- Right actions are naturally performed.
- Obstacles are easily overcome.
- Debilitating subconscious conditionings and addictive tendencies are resisted, weakened, and removed by the superior influences of sustained superconscious states. The psychic (soul) forces formerly confined by them are

released and transformed for creative purposes.

• Symptoms of neurosis disappear.
• Physical health improves.
• Appreciation for life is enhanced.
• Experiences, relationships, and circumstances are wholesome and enjoyable.
• Life-enhancing desires are easily satisfied.
• Needs are spontaneously provided for by the universe.
• Unplanned, life-enriching events frequently occur.
• Indications of real prosperity are readily apparent.

Discard the false notion that the material universe is separate from Spirit. A single creative force emanating from omnipresent Consciousness produces various aspects of itself to manifest and sustain the universe. Knowing this, be firmly resolved to live with enlightened understanding in this world.

Choose to Prosper

Always choose what is highest and best for you and for those for whom you are responsible and with whom you relate. (You are actually related to everyone and everything in the universe). Do what you can to harmoniously integrate the spiritual, mental, physical, and environmental components of your life.

1. In your notebook, write a list of restrictions that may be interfering with your desire or endeavors to function effectively and prosper. Decide what you will do to remove those obstacles.

2. Adhere to spiritual practices that you know to be helpful. If you are religious, read the scripture of your choice for inspiration.

3. Cultivate mental skills, intellectual powers, and the ability to think rationally.

4. Maintain your physical health. Exercise regularly. Choose a natural, wholesome diet. Reduce symptoms of stress. Obtain adequate rest and sleep. Healthy, long life will enable you to enjoyably fulfill all of your meaningful purposes. Write your health regimen.

5. Maintain a friendly, supportive relationship with your environment where you live and work and with the universe as a whole.

When one [constantly] thinks about objects of the senses, attachment to them is produced. Attachment causes desire. From frustrated desire, anger arises and confusion is produced. From confusion, memory is impaired, powers of discernment are diminished and one wanders aimlessly. But the person whose mind is disciplined, who moves in the world with the senses controlled and who is free from attachments and aversions, is soon established in peace. That purity of spirit removes one from all sorrow.

– Bhagavad Gita 2.62–65

Are you in earnest? Seize this very minute. What you can do, or dream you can, begin it. Only engage and then the mind grows heated [inspired and concentrated]. Begin, and then the work will be completed.

– Johann Wolfgang von Goethe

The Eight Success Principles That Make Possible the Fulfillment of All of Life's Purposes

When engaged in the performance of our duties and involved in relationships, we may sometimes forget that our most important duty is to successfully fulfill the higher purposes for which we were born into this world. It is important for us to remember that it is only when we are spiritually awake, healthy-minded, and creatively functional that we are most fully alive and our actions are most beneficial.

Although the natural principles or laws that enable us to prosper cannot be confined to a fixed number, in this chapter I have chosen to emphasize eight fundamental principles which, when applied, make possible the fulfillment of all of life's purposes.

Success Principle #1
Inspiration: The Divine Influence that Empowers

Inspiration is an infusion into the mind and body of spiritual influence arising from within the soul. Every soul has an innate urge to have its capacities enlarged, its potential released, its qualities unfolded, its abilities unrestricted, and its awareness clarified and restored to wholeness. Inspiration energizes the mind and body, enables us to perceive possibilities, improves powers of intellectual discernment, unveils intuition that provides insight, and causes us to want to be skillful and accomplished—to express excellence in all of our actions, relationships, and circumstances.

Inspiration often occurs spontaneously because of the soul's impulse to express its qualities. A spark of inspiration may be ignited when we read a book, listen to a song, hear someone speak, or see something that appeals to and arouses the soul. Because inspiration expands our awareness, when we are influenced by it we may feel ourselves to be more than a mind or personality and believe that situations which were formerly considered to be limiting are no longer so. Inspiration draws from within us the best of which we are capable of expressing.

When our goals and purposes are clearly defined, inspiration energizes and motivates us to accomplish them. It cleanses the mind of confusion, banishes pessimism, evokes self-confidence, and strengthens our resolve to discover and investigate higher realities.

Nurture inspiration by maintaining an optimistic mental attitude; prayer and meditation; daily reading of scriptures or other sources of helpful, consciousness-illuminating information; association with others who are inspired and purposeful; and by constant practice of the presence of God. Maintain good health habits. Inspiration flows more freely when the mind and body are receptive and responsive and realistic short-term and long-term goals are being successfully achieved.

Affirm with conviction:

> A free-flowing current of inspiration energizes and illumines my mind, purifies my intellect, unveils my intuition, enlivens my body, and empowers my wisely chosen, skillfully performed actions.

Success Principle #2
Aspiration: Inspired Desire to Accomplish Purposes

To aspire to achieve meaningful goals and purposes is to rise to a higher level of thinking and action. Do your best to improve your skills and live constructively so that these four primary purposes of life will be accomplished:

1. *Learn what your role in life is and play it well.* Ask, "What is life for?", "Why am I in this world?", and "What can I do to be fulfilled and make a useful contribution to others and the planet?" Use your knowledge and abilities wisely. Aspire to excellence—to the very best of which you are capable of being, doing, and experiencing.

2. *Learn to have your life-enhancing desires easily fulfilled.* You have basic needs that should be satisfied so that you can be healthy, happy, and functional. Satisfying them should not involve all of your time and resources. You are not in this world to struggle to merely survive; you are here to live—to participate, learn, and grow to your full potential. Fulfill the desires that enhance your life and enjoy your learning and growing experiences.

3. *Be affluent*: in a continuous flow of resources and supportive events and relationships because of your sustained prosperity consciousness and wisely chosen, appropriate actions.

4. *Be spiritually awake.* Aspire to be Self-realized, fully enlightened, with your awareness liberated from all delusions and illusions. Don't wait until your physical needs are satisfied before aspiring to be Self-realized and engaging in spiritual practices. Integrate (unify, bring together) your thoughts and actions so that all four of the primary purposes of your life can be accomplished as quickly as possible.

As often as necessary, remind yourself that you are a spiritual being—that it is your destiny to be healthy, happy, unrestricted, effective in all of your actions, prosperous, and successful. If you have thoughts or feelings that are in opposition to your aspirations, use your powers of intellectual discernment. Exercise will power. Change the way you think and behave.

Do what you can to quickly accomplish your purposes. If you do not know what to do, visualize your personal circumstances as you desire them to be. Cultivate and creatively use your powers of imagination as described in chapter five of this book.

If creative ideas arise in your mind, apply them. If you can immediately do something or can begin to do something to fulfill your desire, do it. If you do not know what to do, maintain the subjective state of being fulfilled and let the universe bring into your life all that is needed for you to experience the unfoldment of your highest good.

Concentrate only on what is essential to the accomplishment of your purposes. Avoid thoughts, feelings, relationships, conversations, and behaviors which do not directly relate to your goals.

There is an enlivening Power that nurtures the universe and we can learn to cooperate with it. That Power expresses through us to the degree that we are receptive and responsive to It.

Speak only constructive words which clearly define and declare your aspiration.

Affirm with conviction:

I am always fully awake to the truth of my Being and my relationship to the Infinite. Because I remain in tune with the rhythms of Nature, my constructive desires are always easily fulfilled and I am always in the flow of good fortune.

Success Principle #3
Vision: A Clear Perception of Possibilities

What else can we do to live more effectively? At the soul level, we can intuitively "see" and acknowledge the reality of our ideal future. With our intelligence we can make right choices. With our mind we can engage in possibility-thinking and imagine ideal circumstances. With our energy, abilities, and skills we can perform actions which will produce desired results.

There are no external forces or influences which can permanently determine our experiences or circumstances. If our circumstances are oppressive or unsatisfying, they can be changed by choice, an adjustment of viewpoint, visualization, faith, and constructive actions. If we have not been using our mind creatively, if we have not been performing right actions, we have only to change the way we think and act. Our experiences and circumstances will then be in accord with our thoughts and actions.

Affirm with conviction:

> Consciously established in vivid awareness of my
> true nature, knowing that I am included in the whole-
> ness of the infinite field of Consciousness, sustaining
> my vision of ideal possibilities, I use my mind and abili-
> ties wisely and creatively.

Success Principle #4
Education: Acquiring Knowledge to Live Effectively

We can acquire practical knowledge from others who
are wise and we can awaken and unfold our innate knowledge. It is fairly easy to acquire knowledge of how to be
healthy, how to work, how to interact with people, and
how to use money and resources. When we know how to
think constructively and have experienced a degree of
spiritual growth, it is much easier—and more enjoyable—
to live effectively.

To acquire a spiritual education, it is best to learn from
people who are spiritually enlightened and whose lives
reflect their understanding. Learn the laws or principles
that determine desired results and willingly cooperate
with them.

Emotional maturity is essential to living effectively
and successfully. We are emotionally mature when we
cheerfully assume responsibility for our states of awareness, mental states, personal behaviors, and the results
of our actions. An emotionally mature person does not
blame others or external conditions for the incidents of
misfortune they might experience. They will acknowledge
that their experiences and circumstances result from their

states of consciousness and behaviors. If circumstances need to be improved, improve yourself.

Affirm with conviction:

> I enjoy learning and I learn easily. I am keenly interested in the skillful application of my innate knowledge that unfolds and the practical knowledge I acquire. As my knowledge increases and my skills improve, my awareness expands and I am increasingly competent and successful.

Success Principle #5
*Participation: Personal Involvement
That Allows Us to Be Successful*

We are immortal, spiritual beings. Ask these questions: "How am I living my immortal life?"; "What can I do to live my life flawlessly?"

Many people wonder if it is really possible to live a God-centered life and have mundane needs satisfied. Practical advice is found in *The Gospel According to Saint Matthew* (6.33).

> First, seek the kingdom of God and the way of righteousness, and all these things will be added unto you.
> *Modern Interpretation*
> First, seek knowledge and experience of God, and live in harmony with the universal, therefore reliable, principles of causation. Whatever you need will then be provided for you.

We do not need superior powers of intelligence to live correctly—we only need to learn *how* to live, and do it.

Affirm with conviction:

> I willingly participate in life's unfolding processes,
> live with firm resolve, attend to necessary duties, act
> effectively, and meditate regularly. Anchored in the
> Infinite, I am peaceful, productive, and successful.

Success Principle #6
Faith: Conviction That Produces Results

> Now faith is the substance of things hoped for; the
> evidence of things which are not seen.
> By faith we [can] know that the worlds were formed
> by the word [creative power] of God [Consciousness];
> that things perceived through the senses were not made
> of things which are visible.
>   — New Testament / *Hebrews* 11.1 & 3

Faith is firm belief or conviction which is not based on
external evidence. To a person who is unaware of the subjective side of life, who does not yet know that inner causes
produce outer effects and that one's point of view can be
altered to allow insightful perceptions, faith defies logic.
It is considered to be mere wishful thinking, fantasy, or a
superstitious rite indulged in to nurture hope or pacify
the mind. The exercise of faith requires that we be realistic, that we believe in what is possible to be manifested or
experienced.

As our understanding of Consciousness and its
processes improves, heretofore undiscovered realms of
knowledge are revealed. We know more about soul-mind-
body interactions: that our awareness need not be confined to the mind or body; that powers of perception and

intelligence can be improved; and that a Cosmic Mind is responsive to our thoughts and intentions. It is a fact that our sustained beliefs can not only influence our health, the outcomes of our personal endeavors, and the environment—they can definitely cause events, produce circumstances, and attract resources that are desired or needed.

Affirm with conviction:

> It is easy to live by faith. I know that I abide in the boundless field of Infinite Consciousness from which the universe is emanated and by which it is nurtured. I know that what I clearly visualize and can firmly believe to be true, I can definitely experience.

Success Principle # 7
Persistence: Unwavering Dedication to the Ideal

When resolved on a constructive course of action, persist until desired results are experienced. Many people begin worthwhile projects with strong resolve, only to quit too soon or give up too easily. Their faith wavers. Their concentration is faulty. Their will to prevail is weak. When you know that you are on the right course, don't give up. Ignore the negative comments of others. Do not let the word "impossible" enter your mind. Think only about what *is* possible and focus your thoughts and energies on that. Pray for strength and guidance, both of which will emerge from within the depths of your Being. Your consistent performance of wisely chosen, effective actions and the prospering influence of your ever-increasing awareness of the Power that nurtures the universe, and you, will enable you to prevail.

Affirm with conviction:

> I know what is important and I adhere to it with
> unwavering faith and alert, skillful actions. With cheer-
> ful resolve and absolute trust in God I persist until I
> achieve my goals and accomplish my purposes.

Success Principle #8
Grace: the Actions of the Nurturing Impulses
of Consciousness That Make Possible Effortless
Unfoldments of Our Highest Good

By doing our very best to learn, live effectively, and
grow, we unfold our innate knowledge, perfect our skills,
and become more receptive and responsive to the nurturing actions of grace.

The enlivening, redemptive actions of grace are impelled by the evolutionary impulses of Consciousness that
maintain the orderly processes of the universe, contribute to our spiritual awakening and growth, and support
our constructive endeavors. Because grace flows freely, it
is available to everyone. Its actions are effortless and its
effects always result in the highest good.

Affirm with conviction:

> I am prosperous. I live effectively. I am receptive to
> my unplanned good that the universe provides. I am
> always compliantly responsive to the freely expressive
> actions of God's nurturing grace.

Life always provides us with what we ask for and are
able to accept. If life seems to be denying you the good

fortune you desire, perhaps it is because you are consciously or unconsciously withholding yourself from life. Examine your mental and emotional states and your behaviors to discover whether or not you are limiting yourself. If prosperity seems to be avoiding you, perhaps you have not yet asked for it. Perhaps you have asked, but were not able to receive.

Fearlessly ask life for that which you deserve. Expand your capacity to receive. Remove all obstacles to fulfillment and you will surely be fulfilled. Let the Infinite Life flow through you. Prosper in all ways and share your light and your good fortune with others.

Learn These Success Principles

Success principles are impersonal and universal. Use them to quicken your spiritual growth and to prosper in all aspects of your life.

1. Be interested in living; enjoy the experience. Feel the currents of life flowing through you, impelling and *inspiring* you to constructive actions.

2. Ask, "What am I in this world to do, experience, or accomplish?" Write the answers as they surface in your mind, then *aspire* to do, experience, and accomplish. You need not ask anyone's permission. Follow the leading of your heart—the innermost level of your Being.

3. What is your *vision* of possibilities? What can you see for yourself and others? How far into the future can you clearly see? Write the possibilities.

4. What knowledge do you yet need to enable you to live effectively? Acquire it. What skills do you need to be able to accomplish your purposes? Acquire, perfect, and use them. *Educate* yourself by exposure to sources of useful information and by calling forth your innate knowledge and abilities. You will live forever in this world or another one. You need never stop learning. To live is to continue to enlarge your capacities.

5. Be willing to *participate* in the game of life. Let yourself grow. Be curious. Be Self- (soul) confident. Be willing to outgrow the limitations of the mind and personality and see through delusions and illusions to what is real and of value. The processes of life are continually flowing. Get in the flow. Let the currents of life effortlessly carry you along.

6. After only a little practice, it is much easier to live by *faith* than to doubt and be fearful. Through eons of time the processes of life have supported, nurtured, and brought you thus far. They will continue to do so. Trust life. Be firm in *faith*.

7. When you are committed to right actions and the fulfillment of your destiny, *persist*. The alternative is not worthwhile. View obstacles as opportunities to learn. Let challenges bring out your best qualities. As you go more deeply into life, the greater will be your understanding and the more your innate powers will unfold. You will eventually succeed. Why not now?

8. You are not alone in the universe. You are already one with the wholeness of life. Learn to let *grace*, the supportive impulses of Consciousness that enliven all of Nature also enliven and nurture you. It has always been supportive of you even when you have not known it. Its actions will be more evident as you become receptive to them. Be thankful for the good fortune you now have. Welcome unplanned good fortune.

By deep meditation and living a God-centered life, calm the waves of thoughts and desires that condition your perceptions of reality. You will then behold everything as it really is.

– *Paramahansa Yogananda*

CHAPTER FOUR

The Deep Silence That Refreshes the Mind and Spirit

Only a perception of the sacred, of that which evokes a response of veneration or reverent regard, can satisfy the soul and thereby enrich our lives. Without it, though we might possess everything else a person could want in this world, in our quiet moments alone with our thoughts, we know that our lives are barren.

"He is wisest who seeks to know God," my teacher Paramahansa Yogananda once said. "He is the most successful who has realized God."

While endeavoring to apprehend the wholeness of life, we need not withdraw from the world which is included in that wholeness. We need only be selective; choosing that which is pure and which enhances our lives while refraining from what troubles the mind, blurs perceptions, and may contribute to misfortune.

Ordinary self-conscious awareness is clouded, distorted and fragmented because of an almost ceaseless stream of impulses arising from subliminal levels of the mind. These influential impulses arise because of restlessness, discontent, subconscious conflicts, and the force of instinctual urges and tendencies. Of these, restlessness and discontent are more easily remedied. Subconscious conflicts may be more difficult to resolve. Instinctual urges and tendencies to satisfy physical and emotional urges can be disciplined by mastery of attention.

The most effective way to pacify restless thoughts and the subliminal drives that nourish them is to regularly practice superconscious meditation. When correctly and effectively practiced, the procedure elicits physical relaxation, emotions are calmed, thought processes are refined, the forces of subliminal drives are weakened and neutralized, and awareness becomes tranquil and clear. This tranquil, clear, superconscious state is superior to ordinary waking states, sleep states, and unconsciousness.

Preliminary meditative superconscious states may be mixed with subtle thoughts and prevailing moods, causing the meditator to wonder whether or not the predominant calm state is really superconsciousness or merely a more refined state of ordinary awareness. With practice, one acquires the ability to observe subtle thoughts and moods with objectivity, then banish them by a gentle act of will (an impulse of intention) or ignore them and allow them to eventually subside.

Repeated practice soon enables the alert meditator to discern and experience the difference between the permanent, real pure conscious nature (the essence of Being) and the conflicted, fragmented states common to ordinary states of awareness. When this difference is recognized, by attentive practice it is possible to choose to be established in awareness of Being at all times, even when engaged in activities and relationships. Perceptions are then more accurate; intellectual powers are enhanced; intuition is more reliable; and actions are performed skillfully and effectively with less effort.

Beginning meditators are advised to remember that

the primary purpose of meditation practice is to discern and experience the truth of their Being; know the eight stages of preparation and practice; and practice correctly and regularly until the primary purpose of practice is accomplished.

The Eight Stages of Preparation and Practice

1. *Ethical living.* Personal conduct that produces and maintains orderly, supportive relationships with others and the environment provides a firm foundation which supports purposeful living and spiritual growth. The five fundamental behavioral guidelines to which to conform are: harmlessness in thought and deed; truthfulness; honesty; disciplined use of the senses, thoughts, energy, and actions for entirely constructive purposes; nonaddictive, right use of material things and resources. As spiritual growth progresses, no effort is required to conform to these behaviors; they are spontaneously expressed by the innate inclinations of the soul.

2. *Adherence to practices which contribute to physical well-being, psychological transformation, and rapid spiritual growth.* Keep your body clean and healthy. Learn to be patient and soul-satisfied in all circumstances while doing what you can to improve, change, or transcend oppressive circumstances. To effect psychological transformation, choose to be emotionally mature by being responsible for your thoughts, moods, behaviors, actions, and the results of your actions. Study and intellectually and intuitively analyze the nature of Consciousness and its processes until you acquire insight and clearly know the facts about it, yourself, and your relationship to life.

Surrender (let go of) your illusional sense of selfhood in favor of apprehending and experiencing the truth of Being.

3. *Sitting*. In a quiet place, where you will not be disturbed, sit upright on a chair or in a cross-legged posture, whichever is most comfortable for you. While it is all right, when meditating, to adjust your position whenever necessary for the purpose of comfort, avoid unnecessary movements because of restlessness. Close your eyes. Gaze gently into the space between your eyebrows. Remember that the primary purpose of meditation practice is to become aware of your pure conscious nature. If you pray, acknowledge God in your usual way and pray briefly to attune yourself to the reality of the Presence of God.

4. *Freeing and balancing the flows of life force in the body to elicit relaxation and calm the actions of the mind*. This can be accomplished in a variety of ways. Contemplate the chosen object of concentration or practice a meditation technique with alert attention.

5. *Internalization of attention*. The meditator's awareness is now completely withdrawn from the body, senses, moods, and thought processes.

6. *Concentration*. Attention is fully directed to the meditation object or ideal.

7. *Meditation*. Experienced when attention flows smoothly: intentionally directed by the meditator; spontaneously because of the attractiveness of the meditation object or ideal; or as determined by the soul's innate impulse to have its awareness restored to wholeness.

8. *Superconsciousness*. Clarified awareness, which may be experienced with the support of the meditative object or as pure existence-Being without the support of a meditative object.

Helpful Guidelines to Effective Meditation Practice

• Meditate once or twice a day on a regular schedule. Early morning after restful sleep, while thoughts and emotions are still subdued, is recommended. Early morning practice confers three practical benefits: (1) procrastination is avoided; (2) after meditation practice you will be more alert and purposeful; (3) you will be more self-confident because of knowing that you have done something to confirm your intention to live effectively. If early morning practice is not possible, any time you choose will be suitable. *Note:* For some people, who feel tired or whose awareness is blurred when they awake from sleep, early morning is not the best time for them to meditate. If physical or psychological problems contribute to early morning tiredness or inability to concentrate, actions should be implemented to resolve the problem.

• Short sessions (15 to 20 minutes) to elicit relaxation and refresh the mind and spirit are beneficial.

• Longer sessions (30 minutes to an hour) will enable you to go beyond the preliminary stages of practice and experience more refined superconscious states. If longer sessions cannot be scheduled daily, schedule them weekly, biweekly, or monthly.

• Meditate with alert attention. Avoid passive sitting, daydreaming, and sleep. Meditate with purpose. Be curious about the process. Be attentive to what you are doing and to what is occurring. Aspire to be spiritually awake. Nurture devotion to God. Let your awareness blend into and merge with formless, infinite Consciousness.

• When necessary, use a meditation technique.

• When awareness is clear and tranquil, discontinue the

use of a meditation technique. Let superconscious states spontaneously emerge.

• Ignore all physical sensations, memories, thoughts, moods, and illusory meditative perceptions.

Meditation Techniques to Learn and Skillfully Use

A technique is a systematic procedure used to solve a problem or accomplish a purpose. Attentive practice of meditation techniques will enable you to observe, experience, and understand soul-mind-body relationships and their interactions.

Experiment: Before actively engaging in meditation practice, sit quietly for several minutes. Observe your thoughts, moods, breathing pattern, and physical states. Notice the relationship between the speed and forcefulness of breathing and your thoughts, moods, and physical states. As you relax, your breathing pattern becomes slower and less forceful, thoughts are more orderly, and your emotions are calmed.

You did not have to do anything to cause these effects; they occurred naturally. Likewise, when meditating, there is no need to contend with random thoughts, memories, or shifting moods. They will automatically become calm, then dormant when attention is concentrated on the purpose of your practice.

A meditation technique may not be needed when devotion-empowered aspiration to be Self-realized is strong. Simply sitting, waiting and watching, may be sufficient. Or you can pray to be aware of the Presence of God, then patiently wait, alert and attentive, in the deep silence. Meditation may then flow smoothly. If concentration is distracted by mental or emotional states, skillful use of a meditation technique can be extremely helpful.

A mantra—a word, a word-phrase, or a sound—may be used to focus attention. For most meditators, during the early stages of practice before meditation flows spontaneously, listening to a mantra is more helpful than "waiting and observing" because it supports concentration. Until awareness without the support of an object of concentration is easy to maintain, the force of habit may incline the meditator to identify awareness with thoughts, memories, feelings, fantasies, semiconscious states of reverie, or sleep. When attention is fully identified with a mantra, because thoughts, memories, and emotions are ignored, they diminish in intensity and eventually become dormant. When awareness is calm and tranquil, the mantra can be ignored. Superconsciousness will then prevail.

A mantra should be a word or sound that is pleasant to use; attention will then be easily attracted to it. For beginning meditators, any agreeable word is suitable, such as *peace*, *joy*, or *God*. If English is not your primary language, use words which have similar meanings in the language you ordinarily use. For instance, instead of the word *peace* a follower of Judaism might prefer the Hebrew word *shalom*, while a Hindu might prefer *shanti*.

A word-phrase mantra may be used. *Om-God* is popular with many meditators, as is the Sanskrit mantra *so-hum*. When you have success with a mantra, use it regularly. Its familiarity will make it comfortable to use and memories of past enjoyable meditation sessions during which that mantra was used will elicit a similar response. If, after several weeks or months, a mantra loses its appeal, use another one that will enable you to remain alert and attentive.

If you are a new meditator, while it may be helpful to be personally instructed and encouraged by an experienced meditator, the information in this chapter provides all you need to know to practice with benefit. There is no need to pay hundreds of dollars to learn this simple process or to learn a "special" technique. When the meditation process is known, you have only to practice on a regular schedule to acquire proficiency and experience the beneficial changes that will occur.

Mantra meditation is not a hypnotic procedure. A mantra is used only to focus attention and avoid distractions. When meditating, remain alert. Allow at least twenty minutes to practice the following routine:

1. Sit upright. Close your eyes. Flow your attention to the space between and above your eyebrows. Pray silently, or sit quietly for a few moments. Remember that you are a spiritual being abiding in the ocean of Infinite Consciousness and that the primary purpose of meditation practice is to clarify your awareness.

2. If meditation flows spontaneously, let it happen. If it does not, use a helpful meditation technique to elicit relaxation and mental and emotional calmness. If you use a single word mantra, mentally recite it when you inhale, experience peacefulness when you exhale. As you progress, instead of mentally reciting the mantra, mentally "listen" to it. Have no anxiety about the outcome of practice. Avoid effort. Be attentive.

3. When you are poised, and your awareness is clear and tranquil, neglect the mantra and rest in that calm, aware state until you are inclined to conclude the ses-

sion. Retain your meditative calm as you turn your attention outward to resume your ordinary activities. Be happy. Feel thankful.

When using a word-phrase (examples: *Om-God* or *so-hum*) use the first word with inhalation and the second word with exhalation. This can also be done with a single word that has two syllables. As breathing becomes slow and refined, mental processes and emotional states are less forceful. As your practice progresses, you may remove your attention from the breath and listen to the mantra until it fades and vanishes. If concentration wavers after use of the mantra has been discontinued, use it again to focus your attention. Sometimes, at this stage of practice, an act of gentle intention will enable you to remain concentrated without the use of a technique.

By repeated practice of meditation to the stage of tranquil awareness of Being, superconscious states are progressively refined. Their superior influences weaken and neutralize addictive tendencies and destructive subconscious conditionings, organize mental processes, purify the intellect, and illumine the meditator's field of awareness. In the course of time, superconsciousness blends with and transforms ordinary states of self-conscious awareness, unveiling the soul's intuitive powers and allowing cosmic consciousness—perception of the wholeness of life—to be the normal state. Although there have been reported instances of sudden awakening to cosmic consciousness, they are rare; it is more usual that it emerges gradually.

When meditating, if you experience pleasant moods, blissful sensations, or perceptions of light, enjoy them if you want to, without becoming attached to them. What you perceive as other than you (Being) is not you. The bliss to which enlightened meditators refer is not an emotion or sensations of energy flows in the body; it is the pure joy of clear perception of Being.

Preliminary meditative light perceptions, similar to the perceptions sometimes reported by people who have experienced a near-death episode, may occur. When the body's life forces flow back to the brain, brain centers that produce the lights and sometimes produce sensations of peace, unity-consciousness, and transcendence are influenced. Recent research indicates that beatific visions and transcendent perceptions are associated with electrical stimulation and blood flows and blockages involving the prefrontal cortex and other lobes of the brain. Even if some meditative perceptions and sensations are brain-related, they can be used to internalize attention, then be transcended. Do not become attached to them or err in believing that when they occur (if they do) that you are talking with God. Beyond brain-related perceptions is the reality of Consciousness.

Spiritual growth without a prosperity consciousness is not possible. Like the evidential expressions of prosperity in all other aspects of our lives, the enlargement of soul capacities can only be experienced when spiritual, mental, physical, and environmental components of life are harmoniously integrated. To become aware of and unfold our innate potential to be knowledgeable and freely functional, we have to be receptive to these conditions.

Tenacious attachment to conditioned self-centered states of consciousness fragmented by delusions and illusions, and to behaviors and personal relationships which reinforce them, interferes with spiritual growth. Egocentricity contracts and confines awareness. For authentic spiritual growth to occur, awareness has to be clarified, expanded, and unconfined.

Awakening Through the Stages of Spiritual Growth

Seven levels of soul awareness indicate the stages through which souls progressively awaken to Self- and God-realization.

1. *Restricted self-consciousness.* Mental dullness, apathy, self-centeredness, and boredom are common characteristics. Awareness is fully identified with the physical body and personality. Endeavors are mostly directed to physical survival, mundane concerns, and perpetuation of one's limited view of self. Activities and relationships are ordinary, as necessary or as one is inclined by needs, desires, or whims. Intellectual powers are weak. Memories, habits, and acquired behaviors determine actions and experiences. Provincialism (small-mindedness) may prevail. If one is religious, commonly accepted (or superstitious) beliefs that comfort the mind or support one's lifestyle may be considered to be more important than knowledge. Prayer is usually directed to an imagined, personalized form of God.

2. *Dysfunctional self-consciousness.* Mental confusion and conflicted emotional states are common characteristics. Egocentricity that contracts awareness nurtures delusions, illusions, obsessions, fantasies, sentiment without discernment, emotional dependency, addictions, and habitual debilitating behaviors. Thoughts, speech, and behaviors are often irrational. One may be neurotic and

judgmental, or complain, blame, find fault, or refuse to be responsible for personal behaviors. Subconscious conditionings and subliminal influences are powerfully influential. The approval of others may be believed to be important. Because intellectual powers are not yet fully developed, fascination with psychic phenomena, mediumship (channeling), endeavors to recall previous incarnations, hypnosis or other mind-conditioning practices, and systems which may be advertised as shortcuts to enlightenment, may interfere with effective living and aspiration to be spiritually awake.

3. *Functional self-consciousness.* A healthy-minded, superior self-conscious state. Experiences and relationships are wholesome and constructive. Purposeful actions are performed skillfully. One may have partial intellectual comprehension of spiritual realities and be interested in self-improvement and spiritual growth. Because awareness is still somewhat ego-centered, one's interest in spiritual matters may be tinged with self-serving inclinations.

4. *Superconsciousness.* A partial or advanced degree of Self-realization with knowledge that one is an individualized aspect of the boundless field of Consciousness along with sincere aspiration to be fully awake. Actions are skillfully performed. Activities and relationships are enjoyably experienced. Subconscious conditionings are only mildly influential. Powers of intellectual discernment and intuitive perception are well-developed. Behaviors are ethical and appropriate.

5. *Cosmic Consciousness.* Partial or complete awareness of the wholeness of life. If this state is only partially experienced, so long as it is nurtured it continues to gradually emerge. Thoughts are orderly and creative. Per-

ceptions are clear and accurate. Joy-permeated soul contentment is constant. Innate knowledge of Consciousness and its processes unfolds.

6. *God Consciousness.* Partial or complete realization of the wholeness of Consciousness and its categories of manifestations. If mental restrictions are present, they are rapidly weakened and removed.

7. *Complete Enlightenment.* The final, fully awake, soul-liberated state. Awareness is fully restored to wholeness. When relating to the mundane realms, enlightenment is undiminished and all actions are appropriately spontaneous.

Until enlightenment is complete and permanent, some characteristics of all levels of awareness may be present: "saints" may still have a few illusions and error-prone persons may express virtuous qualities. To facilitate rapid spiritual growth, renounce the characteristics and behaviors which are restrictive while cultivating states of consciousness and behaviors which conform to your highest aspirations.

Schedule at least one hour a day for self-care and deep meditation. Attend to your physical wellness routines, nourish your mind with inspired ideas, and meditate deeply until your awareness is calm and clear. If possible, have a quiet, clean place set aside for meditative contemplation. When you go there, put aside all secular concerns. Rest in the deep silence until your mind is refreshed, your awareness is clear, and soul contentment prevails.

Meditate Regularly and Live
With Conscious Intention

Whenever you sit to meditate, remember that the primary purpose of meditation practice is to clarify and restore your awareness to wholeness.

At the core of your Being, you are peaceful; you know that you are a spiritual being abiding in the wholeness of God. By removing your awareness from physical sensations and mental processes, you can consciously be aware of what you already are.

1. To experience the practical benefits of meditation practice—physical relaxation, stress reduction, peace of mind, orderly thinking, a stronger immune system, slowing of biologic aging processes, increased energy, and improved powers of perception—meditate once or twice daily for fifteen to twenty minutes. Short, alert meditation practice sessions are more beneficial than longer, passive sessions.

2. As your meditation skills improve, sit longer until superconscious states emerge and meditation flows smoothly, impelled by your innate urge to be fully awake—Self- and God-realized.

3. Be patient. Results will occur naturally.

4. Conscious, intentional living is spiritual practice. Meditation practice requires but a small portion of the time you have each day to experience your life. By self-training, learn to always be alert and attentive. You will then live superconsciously, without delusions or illusions clouding or fragmenting your awareness.

5. Have a daily routine. After restful sleep, attend to your morning self-care regimen, meditate, then turn your attention to the day's schedule of activities.

6. Do everything skillfully. Respect and nurture the innate divine nature of every person and living thing. Avoid meaningless or superficial social involvements.

7. Whenever you become distracted, confused, or moody, withdraw for a few minutes. Be still until your mind is calm and you are again soul-centered.

8. In the afternoon or evening, meditate a few minutes for inner refreshment. Ponder your relationship with the Infinite as you go to sleep. If you should awaken during the night, be still and enjoy the deep silence.

Shall not the heart which has received so much, trust the Power by which it lives? May it not quit other leadings, and listen to the Soul which has guided it so gently, and taught it so much, secure that the future will be worthy of the past?

– Ralph Waldo Emerson

CHAPTER FIVE

What You Can Clearly Imagine and Believe, You Can Experience

When our awareness is established in Being, our change-less true nature, we are at peace. Our thoughts, moods, and actions are well-ordered and spontaneously appropriate and personal relationships and circumstances are supportive and satisfying. Timely events occur in an uninterrupted flow. Resources, in whatever form they are needed, are readily available. When these ideal conditions do not prevail, remedial actions can, and should, be immediately implemented.

The first action to perform is to withdraw attention from external circumstances and from emotional states and random thought processes. The reason for doing this is that, when our awareness is not established in Being, thoughts are inclined to be disorganized, emotions may interfere with our attempts to think rationally, perceptions are blurred, and endeavors to choose a right course of action may be flawed because intellectual powers are impaired. The most common intellectual error we are then liable to make is to presume that our states of consciousness and present and future well-being are totally dependent upon external circumstances and influences.

When we are troubled, when our awareness is clouded and the reality of Being is obscured, or we think or feel ourselves to be victims of circumstances, what is needed is a change of viewpoint that restores our awareness to wholeness. We can then proceed to easily renounce circumstances we do not want and accept only those which are fully supportive of us and our aspiration to excellence.

Until all of our thoughts and actions are spontaneously and appropriately expressive because of our constant realization of Being, we can assist ourselves to spiritual growth and improve our circumstances by various practical means.

Answer this question: How would you live your life if you had abundant resources, unlimited potential, and absolute knowledge that you could always accomplish your purposes? Abundant resources are available to you *now*. You already have unlimited potential within you. You can accomplish your purposes by your right actions.

Speak these words aloud with conviction:

> The possibilities which I can clearly envision, and firmly believe to be true, can occur or be experienced.

For imagination reinforced by faith to be effective, cooperation with natural laws is necessary. All events that occur in time and space, even the uncommon events referred to as miracles, have specific causes. There are no exceptions. To imagine and believe in what is not possible will result in frustration. Passive daydreaming, undefined wishful thinking, and fantasy are not recommended. Inclinations to want to control, manipulate, or cause harm to others are to be avoided. Desires and motives should be pure and selfless.

Imagination reinforced by faith can be applied to:

* Quicken spiritual growth.
* Improve mental skills and intellectual ability.
* Improve powers of intuition.
* Heal psychological conflicts and trauma.
* Heal the physical body.
* Acquire knowledge.
* Unfold innate soul qualities.
* Learn and improve skills.
* Achieve goals and accomplish purposes.
* Manifest or attract supportive circumstances.
* Attract material resources.
* Help others who are in need.
* Nurture the processes of evolution and clarify the collective consciousness of Planet Earth.

Endeavors to accomplish meaningful purposes will be more effective when the principles of cause and effect are understood:

* Gravity causes objects to fall.
* Motionless objects remain motionless unless their inertia is overcome by an influential force.
* Objects in motion continue to move until opposed by a superior force.
* The quantity of energy in the universe is constant; it neither decreases nor increases.
* Energy can be transformed into matter and matter can be transformed into energy.
* The universe is composed of electromagnetic forces.
* Thoughts and pure intention can influence cosmic

forces and cause observable effects.

• A supreme Consciousness (God) exists; the universe is manifested and sustained by its cosmic forces.

• Souls are individualized aspects of Consciousness with innate knowledge of Consciousness and its processes. All souls will awaken to complete realization of the truth of their Being.

• Cosmic Mind is produced by Consciousness.

• All minds are parts of the one Cosmic Mind which is responsive to our habitual states of consciousness, mental states, desires, and intentions.

• We attract—and are attracted to—relationships and events and circumstances which are compatible with our states of consciousness and mental states.

• Events can be caused to occur and circumstances can be manifested by desire and intention.

• Because the universe responds to our desires and needs, the easiest way to have desires fulfilled and needs met is to, with faith, acknowledge them to be already actualized.

> Whatever things [material resources or circumstances] you desire, when you pray, believe that you have received them, and you will have them.
> — New Testament / *Mark* 11.24

Pure intention with conviction produces results. Clearly defined, unwavering intention influences the universe and the universe responds by expressing the desired effects. An act of pure intention is devoid of emotion. For an intention to cause desired effects, all that is required is conviction: calm certainty at the innermost level of Being. Causing desired effects or attracting ideal circumstances by concentrated intention is the way of least effort. When we are established in Being, desires are fulfilled, needs are met, and purposes are effortlessly accomplished because of our appropriate, efficient actions and the timely actions of grace.

Practice this Technique to Clarify
Your Awareness, Imagine Possibilities,
and Nurture Faith

1. Meditate until thoughts and emotions are settled and your awareness is clear and tranquil. Rest in that calm state until it persists. Acknowledge that Cosmic Mind is particularized as your mind. Merge your awareness with Infinite Consciousness.

2. In your mind's eye, form a clear mental picture of the ideal circumstances you desire to have. Imagine how you will feel when the desire is fulfilled. There is no need, at this time, to think about actions to perform or be concerned about how events will transpire to actualize your desire. If you cannot easily visualize your desire as being fulfilled, *feel* the fulfillment that will be yours.

3. Remain in the state of realized fulfillment until your conviction of it is unwavering.

4. Conclude the practice session.

If ideas about what you can do to assist your desire to be fulfilled arise in your mind, write them in your private journal. Write your specific action-plans and act decisively. If you do not know what to do, or cannot do anything, be unwavering in your faith that the universe can and will provide the resources and events that are needed to manifest ideal circumstances.

Creative imagination differs from fantasy only in degree. Creative imagination is controlled mental imagery with specific intention. Fantasy is random, unregulated imagination.

This technique is not to be thought of as a practice to be used to further condition the mind; use it to be more fully awake, perceptive, and Self-determined. Practice on a regular schedule until you are permanently established in awareness of Being and always in the flow of resources and supportive events and circumstances.

When Necessary, Also Perform Wisely
Chosen Constructive Actions

Spiritual growth can be accelerated by sustained aspiration to be Self-realized; mastery of attention; clarification of awareness; nurturing psychological transformation and emotional maturity; and other practices which contribute to overall health, refine the brain, and enliven the nervous system. Spiritual growth may be slow, gradual and progressive, or rapid. Results of right endeavor are in accord with one's capacity and willingness to learn and to apply helpful procedures. Right, attentive living is the most useful spiritual practice because it requires that alert attention be directed to essential matters and that behaviors be in accord with the causative principles which determine the fulfillment of purposes.

For a person who is otherwise healthy and capable of performing ordinary duties, the primary obstacle to spiritual growth is complacent self-centeredness. To be self-centered is to have awareness identified with an illusional sense of selfhood. To be Self-aware is to be spiritually awake. Note the difference between the meaning of the words *self* and *Self*. A lower case s̲ indicates that the word is used to refer to an illusional sense of selfhood supported by belief and feeling that one is a mind-personality physical being. An upper case S̲ indicates that the word is used to refer to the essence of Being. When the illusional sense of selfhood is replaced by alert awareness of Being, secondary obstacles—the problems and difficulties associated with ordinary egocentric awareness—are easily solved with insightful understanding and constructive actions, or they quickly disappear. If complacency (smug self-satisfaction) in regard to existing restrictive conditions is allowed to persist, spiritual growth will be inhibited.

If desire for spiritual growth is absent, weak, or so mild or inconsistent that one is not impelled to do anything to fulfill it, spiritual growth will still occur slowly with the passage of time because the innate urge of the soul to be fully conscious and expressive will eventually prevail over all obstacles.

Possibility-thinking, attentive use of creative imagination, and faith will definitely contribute to spiritual awakening and rapid unfoldment of innate knowledge and qualities. Imagine how it would be to be fully enlightened: devoid of delusions and illusions, with total comprehension of Infinite Consciousness and its processes and limitless freedom to thrive, flourish, and be successful in all of your meaningful endeavors. Doing this will provide you with subjective awareness of what it is like to be enlightened. It will enable you to shift your point of view, to be egoless and problem-free. Your awareness will be clear.

Mental skills and intellectual ability can be improved by more effectively using the skills you have. The mind, of which the brain is the material organ, processes information. The intellect is the faculty of discernment. You are neither mind nor intellect; you are a spiritual being superior to both.

To acquire the ability to direct attention at will, an attitude of dispassionate objectivity is helpful. Calmly centered in Being, observe your feelings, urges, inclinations, and thoughts with detachment. Choose the feelings, urges, inclinations, and thoughts you want to allow to be expressive. Pacify those which are not compatible with your choices. Allow only orderly, rational thought processes to occur. Refuse to allow sentiment, habit, or emotions to determine your thinking. When communicating with others, speak (or write) with specific intention. Your thinking will then be more rational.

Never believe or say that you cannot think clearly; have a faulty memory; cannot comprehend what you read, hear, or see; or that your intellectual powers are weak. Affirm only that which you desire to be true for you. Improve your ability to think clearly, access memories, comprehend information, accurately perceive, solve problems, and discern the facts about what you are intellectually pondering.

Maintain a healthy lifestyle, balancing activities with rest. Erratic lifestyle routines, physiological imbalance, poor nutrition, insufficient sleep, and tiredness can result in mental confusion, inability to concentrate, emotional instability, and impaired intellectual capacities. Avoid worry, anxiety, restlessness, impatience, and purposelessness. When tired, confused, overstressed, or overwhelmed with challenges, set aside a weekend or several days to rest more than usual. Allow your energies to be renewed and your mind to be refreshed. Eat lightly, read inspirational literature, pray gently, meditate peacefully.

Use creative imagination to "see" and feel yourself to be alert, mentally skillful, rational, curious, observant, and intellectually discerning. Envision and feel your mind to be one with Cosmic Mind. Blend your awareness with Infinite Consciousness. Be secure, confident, and capable.

Intuition can be developed by nurturing mental calmness and emotional stability and by cultivating intellectual proficiency and clarity of awareness. Intuition is sometimes referred to as extrasensory perception independent of the mind and senses. When our awareness is not blurred, it is possible to "know by knowing."

The intellectual faculty is a material organ of perception. When purified, it enables mental concepts and gross aspects of Nature to be comprehended. Subtle aspects of Nature and of nonphysical realities which cannot be perceived by the senses can only be intuitively apprehended. One of the reasons why many people have difficulty in grasping philosophical concepts and understanding higher orders of reality is that their intellectual and intuitive powers have not yet been fully developed. They may, because of their faith, be able to experience a measure of benefit because of their constructive living practices, yet lack the capacity to have knowledge of why and how the processes of Consciousness function as they do. Living constructively as an act of faith is better than doing otherwise. It is more satisfying and consciousness-liberating to live constructively with awareness and knowledge of the truth of Being and the wholeness of life.

Use the technique of creative imagination to order your thoughts, calm your emotions, and clarify your awareness. Intuitive abilities will naturally unfold.

Psychological conflicts and trauma can be healed by right Self-identity, rational thinking, attitude adjustment and behavior modification along with emphasis on purposeful, constructive living. If the causes of mental and emotional disturbance and/or trauma are known, they can be viewed dispassionately, and their influences weakened and neutralized. If misunderstanding is a primary cause, insight will heal the condition. If self-forgiveness is needed, accept it. If there is a need to forgive others, forgive them. If erroneous ideas and beliefs are troublesome, replace them with knowledge. If illusions and fantasies have been allowed to persist, cease from illusory thinking and fantasy. When feeling overwhelmed by pain which accompanies unpleasant memories, breathe more deeply than usual for a minute or two. The pleasure-sensation of breathing will help to keep your attention focused in the present moment.

Avoid preoccupation with unpleasant memories. Past actions cannot be changed; only present and future actions can be chosen and performed. Avoid talking about personal problems. When possible, associate with healthy-minded, idealistic, purposeful friends and associates. If the causes of psychological unrest are unknown, there is no need to obsessively explore the hidden realms of the mind. It is more useful to have a clear sense of meaningful purpose for your life and direct your attention and energies to the accomplishment of it. Choose your course of action and adhere to it. Support your resolve to be happy and functional by adopting a healthy lifestyle.

Use creative imagination to elicit a state of awareness in which you are problem-free and psychologically healthy. Maintain your mental clarity and emotional peace after the practice session. Whenever you notice that your attention is unfocused, or thought processes or moods tend to dominate your awareness, recall the Being-centered state of awareness that prevailed when you used the technique effectively and identify with that experience.

Physical healing can be facilitated by nurturing psychological health and spiritual awareness, adopting lifestyle regimens which allow the forces of Nature to be supportive, and balancing the basic mind-body constitution. The subtle governing principles which regulate physiological processes are influenced by mental and emotional states, behaviors, food, and prevailing environmental factors. Train yourself to think, feel, and act constructively. Establish a regular exercise routine that is compatible with your basic mind-body constitution. Hatha yoga practice and t'ai chi routines are excellent. Choose simple nutrition-rich foods. Maintain ideal body weight. Have a wholesome living and work environment. Associate only with healthy-minded people. Pray, then meditate to the stage of superconscious awareness every day. Regenerative soul forces will flow through your mind and body. If professional help is needed, work with someone who is knowledgeable, skillful, and spiritually aware.

Use imagination to clarify your awareness, then assume an attitude and feeling of total wellness. Maintain that attitude and feeling after the practice session. While doing all of the practical things you know to be helpful, have faith that your spiritual awareness is superior to physical conditions.

Practical knowledge can be acquired by learning from others and by personal experience. Innate knowledge is not acquired; it unfolds from within the core of our Being. Be willing to learn from others who are knowledgeable. Apply what you learn. Knowledge that is not applied is only information.

Use imagination to transcend thoughts or feelings of inability to learn or to know. Rest in the silence, at the seat of all knowledge, then use the knowledge you have to live effectively and accomplish your purposes. Acquired knowledge will blend with Self-revealed knowledge. Your functional skills will improve and the wholeness of life will be directly apprehended. You will become increasingly cosmic conscious.

Innate soul qualities spontaneously unfold when mental and physical restrictions which confine them are removed. These restrictions can be removed by practices which nurture mental and emotional health and spiritual growth. Use imagination to "see" and feel yourself to be free from all restrictions. Assist the awareness-clearing process by thinking rationally, cultivating emotional peace, and regular practice of superconscious meditation.

Functional skills can be improved by effective, self-confident living. Competence is the result of applying knowledge and abilities. Use imagination to improve self-confidence. Be willing to play the game of life successfully. Regardless of your calendar age, be willing to learn new skills. Contrary to opinions thought to be true many years ago, intellectual powers need not diminish with the passage of time. Be innovative. Acquiring new information and performing new or different actions expands awareness and opens pathways in the brain.

Worthwhile goals and purposes can be achieved by visualizing them as being already achieved and by performing actions which may be necessary for their actualization. Imagine circumstances as they will be when your goals and purposes are actualized. Be sure to elicit the feelings which correspond with the end result. For instance, if you want to travel to a distant destination but do not have enough money to pay for the trip, imagine yourself to be already there. Feel the satisfaction that you will feel when you are there. Financial resources or other supportive circumstances will be made available to you, easily and naturally.

Others who are in need of help can be assisted. If you know of someone who is in need, adjust your awareness until you experience wholeness, then know the person to be included in that wholeness. Work on their behalf for the highest good, without endeavoring to manipulate them or their circumstances. If positive results immediately occur, be thankful. If results are not forthcoming, do not despair. You have done your part. When assisting others, offer to provide them useful information they can use to help themselves.

Our spiritual awareness enlivens the processes of evolution and clarifies the collective consciousness of the planet. While it is useful to do practical things to nurture the environment and provide the means by which others can learn to be functional and spiritually aware, our most helpful contribution to the world is to be spiritually awake.

If you put your will on the side of victory, the whole of the universe puts itself behind your will, releases it, reinforces it, redeems it—and you.

– *E. Stanley Jones*

CHAPTER SIX

How to Use Affirmations Effectively

Speak these words with conviction:

> I am an aware, vital, healthy-minded, immortal spiritual being with unlimited potential to live freely, enjoyably, and effectively.

When you spoke, was your voice vibrant? Or were the words hollow and meaningless? Speak it until you *feel* and *know* that you are in full command of your thoughts, feelings, senses, and states of consciousness.

The purpose of intentional affirmation is not to further condition or program the subconscious level of mind, create a pleasant mood, or arouse mild hope that what is affirmed *may* eventually happen. Self-defeating mental habits and personal behaviors, emotional conflicts, and addictive tendencies will automatically be corrected when soul awareness is more pronounced, higher understanding is acquired, and self-confidence nurtured by successful living is constant. Mechanical repetition of affirmations is a waste of time. Speak with deliberate, soul-felt conviction until superconscious awareness of the reality of that which is affirmed is clear and unwavering.

The *master key* to effective use of clearly defined affirmations is to persist until you experience a discernible adjustment of awareness that removes all sense of limitation—until you are firmly established in absolute realization in conformity with the words. When using affirmations, rather than endeavor to use will power to make something happen, remember that personal circumstances invariably correspond to your mental states and states of consciousness. What you think, feel, or know yourself to be capable of experiencing, manifests circumstances and events, attracts them to you, or enables you to perceive them as being presently available.

Affirmations used in this way elicit a transformative, superconscious response. The purpose of using affirmations is to awaken from involvements with thoughts, ideas, and feelings which restrict soul awareness so that desirable circumstances, which are first envisioned as possibilities, are perceived and experienced in fact.

When your awareness is no longer involved with habitual ways of thinking and perceiving, you are free to think rationally and to see possibilities for having ideal circumstances in your life. Always think in terms of your relationship with the Infinite which is without limitations or boundaries. At the deepest level of your being, know yourself to be one with God's all-pervading consciousness which can be experienced as a real, supportive Presence. Act in cooperation with the inclinations of the universe to be supportive of you. When you experience a positive change of mental attitude and are established in soul awareness, endeavor to maintain that Self-realization. This is more easily accomplished by gentle, alert intention. Don't struggle to do this. Effort is a symptom of self-conscious endeavor to force something to happen. Concentrate on *Being*, rather than on becoming; on having, rather than on not having.

When you are established in Self-awareness, you are soul-fulfilled. If there are specific circumstances you want to manifest—physical healing, improved relationships, information you need to acquire, better environmental conditions, more congenial working conditions, elimination of addictive tendencies or harmful or inappropriate behaviors, more evidence of affluence in your life—do what you can to assist the manifestation process. Let the attracting power of your thoughts and states of consciousness bring the experience, events, resources, people, and circumstances which are for your highest good.

With practice, you will discover that *something else* is constructively influential in providing for your needs and total well-being; the actions of God's grace will be increasingly evident. Grace cannot be earned; it can be experienced when you are receptive and responsive to it.

- Sit quietly, alone, where you will be undisturbed.
- Acknowledge your innate, divine nature.
- Acknowledge God's Presence in, as, and around you.
- Speak the affirmation aloud, in a firm, clear voice, with alert intention and soul-felt conviction.
- Repeat it aloud a few times. Let your thoughts, feelings, and awareness conform to the affirmation.
- Affirm a few more times, in a quieter tone of voice.
- Whisper the affirmation a few times, taking it deeper into your consciousness.
- Affirm the affirmation mentally, taking it more deeply within and contemplating its essence.
- Continue to mentally affirm until the affirmation fades and realization of its essence remains. Rest in conviction and realization.

An Alternate Affirmation Practice

- Speak the affirmation aloud with soul-felt conviction until you experience a change of mental attitude and awareness, then maintain those constructive states.
- If you have difficulty with the process, stand in front of a mirror and observe yourself as you speak. Stand tall. Dramatize self-confidence and quiet enthusiasm.

Affirmations for Specific Purposes

For spiritual awakening and growth:

As a perfect expression of God's consciousness, all knowledge of God and of the processes of life is within me. I readily do whatever is necessary to facilitate my complete spiritual awakening and growth. At the innermost level of my being, I am whole. In tune with the Infinite, I am always fully conscious, peaceful, and in harmony with the rhythms of life.

For rational thinking:

My mind is a portion of Universal Mind, the Mind of God. I am always cheerful and optimistic, think clearly, and easily make wise decisions. Knowing that Universal Mind is always responsive to my mental states, states of consciousness, and desires, I allow only entirely constructive urges, thoughts, desires and mental images to arise in my mind.

For emotional stability:

Steadfast in Self-awareness, I am always mentally peaceful and emotionally calm. Because I enjoy living, I easily and appropriately relate to others and to unfolding events. I am attentive every moment with understanding and grace. I am happy. I am thankful.

For coming to terms with painful memories:

Poised in Self-knowledge in relationship to God, I view memories of past events with calm objectivity. When necessary, I easily forgive others and myself. Released from thoughts and feelings of blame, regret, shame, or guilt, I live joyously fulfilled in the present and look forward with anticipation to the wonderful future.

For physical health and well-being:

Knowing that I am an immortal spiritual being, I do everything helpful to allow myself to express freely through my mind and body. I am now receptive and responsive to the radiant, nourishing influences of the cosmic life-forces and energies which nurture, regenerate, and sustain my physical form.

For supportive relationships:

I see the universe as a manifestation of God's cosmic forces. I see all people as divine beings and relate to them with spiritual love and respect. I accept supportive relationships easily and thankfully while being supportive of others and of Nature.

For accomplishment of chosen purposes:

I always skillfully and effectively perform only constructive actions. Envisioning successful outcomes with
unwavering Self-confidence and flawless faith, I wisely
use my abilities to accomplish only meaningful purposes. Fully cooperating with the enlivening Power that
nurtures the universe, I see my highest good and thankfully accept it.

For having a prosperity consciousness:

Because I know that my prosperity is the result of
the harmonious interactions of the spiritual, mental,
physical, and environmental components of life, I am
always attentive to being spiritually aware, mentally
alert, physically healthy, effectively functional, and to
appropriately relating to the world in which I abide.

Help Yourself to Fulfillment

- You know your needs. Clearly define them. Be specific. Choose and affirm only that which is for your highest good. Write and use your own affirmations.
- Embody the ideals defined by your affirmations.
- When you see new opportunities, examine them to be
sure they are what you want, and are the best ones for
you and for others who may be influenced.

Expand Your Awareness

Use creative imagination to increase your capacities to perceive, comprehend, and experience your highest good and to assist others to the highest good which they are capable of experiencing.

1. Do not use creative imagination or will power to try to make something happen. Use it to perceive that which is possible.

2. Patient, right practice will enable you to assume a point of view and a state of consciousness that will enable you to: (1) perform effective actions to cause desired effects; (2) perceive that which you desire as being readily available to you; (3) attract resources and favorable events, relationships, and circumstances.

3. If you are unable to imagine ideal circumstances, imagine and feel that you are fulfilled. Circumstances will conform to your imaginal states and conviction. You may discover that life can provide for you better than what you can imagine. Always imagine end results— what your awareness will be and how you will feel when you are completely fulfilled.

Manifest plainness [be natural], embrace simplicity, reduce selfishness, have few desires.

– Lao-tsu

CHAPTER SEVEN

Money: What It Is, and How to Manage It

Money is a commodity (something considered to be of value) used to conveniently pay for things or services considered to be of equivalent value. The origin of the word *money* is the Latin word *Moneta*, an epithet (descriptive substitute name) for *Juno*, the mythical goddess whose temple in ancient Rome housed the mint where the government's coins were manufactured. Thought of as the wife of the god Jupiter, Juno was looked upon as the patroness of marriage and the well-being of women.

Because of its convenience, various forms of money have been used through the centuries. Well over two thousand years ago, in the Middle East and Asia, metal coins were used to pay for things and services. In some more primitive cultures of the world, sea shells and other items were, and perhaps still are, used for these purposes.

Ordinary coins and pieces of printed paper used as money have but minimal value—they *represent* value. Regardless of the form of money, for it to be reliably useful, all who use it must agree on the value that it represents. The value that money represents is established by people in government agencies who are responsible for supervising the manufacture and distribution of money. Today, the value that money represents is often transferred from one bank account to another one by using checks, credit cards, and computers.

The value that money represents changes from time to time. In countries with weak or unstable economic conditions, the value is decreased. Prices for things and services that people need or want are then increased to the equivalent agreed upon value of money. Greed sometimes motivates people to attempt to raise the prices of things and services beyond the level of the value assigned to money. Unsuspecting or needy buyers then often pay more than the fair price.

When using money, remember that its agreed upon value enables you to acquire what you need or want. Avariciousness, a compulsion to acquire and hoard money just to have it, is a symptom of a deeper psychological problem. Possessiveness and greed cause many people to be mean-spirited, selfish, and to feel alienated from others.

Valid Knowledge and Self-Discipline:
the Two Necessities For Effective
Management of Money

Knowledge which supports the premises upon which life choices are made should be valid (well-grounded, logical, verifiable by practical application). Invalid theories and unreasoned opinions are of no value. Acquire only valid knowledge and use it.

The purpose of having money is to be able to pay for what you need, want, or want to accomplish with it. Be in the flow of money and use it wisely without being attached to it or afraid of it. If your needs, wants, or projects are few, your money supply can be modest. If your needs or projects require a larger flow of money, you should have it. Always having an adequate flow of money will not make you prosperous; it is but one indication of your prosperity consciousness and may nurture your awareness of prosperity. Along with always having an adequate flow of money, you also should be healthy, happy, and spiritually awake. Lack of money does not contribute to health, happiness, or spiritual awareness.

The thoughts and feelings we allow to prevail when we think about money and its uses reveals much about ourselves in regard to our emotional maturity and our capacity (or willingness) to think and behave rationally.

• Do we view money for what it is—a symbolic representation of value to be used for practical purposes? Or are we reluctant to try to comprehend its usefulness or learn how to effectively manage it?

• Does the role that money plays in our lives seem too abstract to understand? Or do we understand the role of money and use it effectively?

• Are we afraid that thinking about money, and attracting and using it, will cause us to become materialistic or unspiritual? Or do we easily attract and wisely use it?

• Do we cling to the mistaken opinion that money is the cause of all human misfortune? Money is symbolic; how it is used determines the effects of its use. Things are neither good nor otherwise. It is insatiable desire for and attachment to things that causes psychological damage and other unpleasant consequences.

• Do we think that we may not have the necessary skills to manage money? Or are we willing to use the skills we have and to acquire those which are needed?

• Are we self-centered, apathetic, and habituated to purposeless behaviors? Or are we enthusiastic about living,
expressing, and accomplishing meaningful purposes?

If you are already in a continuous flow of money and
are managing it easily and wisely, enjoy your financial
abundance. If lack of money is a problem, resolve to learn
how to be in the flow of money and other supportive
resources. You have the right to have your needs satisfied
and your wholesome desires fulfilled.

If you have been resisting financial prosperity, examine your thoughts and feelings to discover why you have
been doing this. Cultivate prosperity ideas. Clarify and
expand your awareness. Conform your behaviors to your
prosperity ideas and to your awareness of possibilities that
exist in the wholeness of life.

If you have been nurturing a poverty consciousness
by indulging in moods, negative thinking, purposeless
behaviors, or meaningless relationships, begin now to
cultivate a prosperity consciousness. Even if you are not
always able to maintain an awareness of wholeness, of
having, avoid talking about your fears or feelings of inad-
equacy. Avoid unnecessary association with others who
are complacent in their impoverished circumstances. Read
inspirational books and articles written by prosperous
people. Meditate regularly. Attend to your daily self-care
routine. Engage in constructive endeavors. Remember
that the wholeness of Consciousness includes you and
everything you need.

Be willing to work (perform serviceable actions) to earn
money. Regardless of your age, if you need to work (or
don't need to work, but want to), prepare yourself by

acquiring the knowledge and skills you will need. If necessary, accept any honest job that will enable you to earn money and acquire experience. Adapt to the work environment and do more than you are paid to do. Choose work that enables you to effectively and constructively use your knowledge and skills. It will then be enjoyable, of value to others, and provide you with opportunities for further learning and growth. Rather than working to earn money, the money you earn will be a secondary result of your endeavors. Your work is right for you when you are enthusiastic about it, it benefits others, and it can be performed without excessive effort.

If you are employed and are not earning enough money, if you like what you do, perform more skillfully so that you will deserve, and receive, more money. If it is not possible to earn more money in your present work situation, move on to a better one.

If you are unemployed and need to work, your immediate "work" is to find a job or create one for yourself. Avoid thinking, believing, or saying that there is nothing available for you to do. Make yourself available. Look for opportunities. Magnetize your mind with determination and faith to attract supportive events and circumstances. Cultivate awareness of the Presence of God.

If you are self-employed and your business is not thriving, if the service you provide or product you offer fills a need or is worthwhile, find out what you have to do to manage your business more effectively and immediately implement plans and actions which will produce the desired results. Render quantity and quality service. Use your available funds and other resources wisely. The wholeness of Consciousness is the source of everything.

Trust it. Expect it to provide for you. Do practical things. Serve people and the universe will provide for you. Money will flow to you from the Source of all things through the people you serve and in unplanned ways.

Most money-related problems are due to lack of knowledge of how to manage money and to irrational thinking and behaviors. Effective money-management is not possible without self-disciplined mastery of attention, thoughts, moods, and behaviors. The ability to make and adhere to right choices is evidence of emotional maturity. If you can easily make right choices and adhere to them, money-management, which is only one aspect of effective living, will be easy. If you do not yet have this skill, acquiring it will nurture your emotional growth. The key to mastery of attention, thoughts, moods, and behaviors is to always do what you know to be most meaningful or beneficial and avoid doing that which is not meaningful or beneficial. Memorize this self-evident fact: If you always do what you know you should do, you will always be successful.

View relationships, things, projects, and your actions with dispassionate objectivity. Use your powers of discriminative intelligence. Avoid allowing your thoughts, moods, or behaviors to be determined by whims, impulsiveness, or sentiment blurred by lack of discernment. Until all of your actions are spontaneously appropriate because of your unwavering, clear awareness of Being, cultivate your power of will, your ability to make right choices.

Whenever you think about earning, acquiring, or using money, remember that it represents value that can be converted to pay your bills or to satisfy other needs. Having money can provide you the freedom to do many of the things you want to do.

Earn money by honest endeavors. Accept money that flows to you freely in other ways: as a gift that does not obligate you, or any fortunate incident.

Be thankful that you are in the flow of money and of other resources that enhance your life. If you sometimes think that you have very little for which to be thankful, adjust your point of view. Remind yourself that you are a spiritual being abiding in the wholeness of Consciousness, with limitless potential to experience and express. Be thankful that you know the truth about yourself and your relationship to the Infinite. From time to time, it can be helpful to write a list of all of the things (knowledge, health, fortunate events, supportive circumstances and relationships) you have. Accept what you have with gratitude. What you need or desire that you do not yet have, visualize. Open your mind and Being to the possibility of having it. Do what you can to fulfill your desires. Be certain that what you desire is worthwhile. Avoid wasting time, energy, and creative abilities on nonessentials.

Use money wisely; avoid waste. Don't think or say, "Money isn't important." Money represents value that is important because of its potential to be beneficially used. Don't spend needlessly, thinking, "It's only money—what is it good for if I can't satisfy my whims?" Think of the value that money represents. Use it only for what you need or really want. Money that is saved can be used to satisfy needs and fund future projects.

Take good care of your home, work environment, clothing and other possessions, and things you use. Think in terms of quality rather than an unnecessary quantity of things. Have whatever you need to be comfortable and to live efficiently. Appropriately relate to and wisely use material things without strong mental or emotional attachment to them. All of your material possessions will eventually wear out, be sold or given away when you no longer need or want them, or will have to be renounced when you leave this world. If you have aversions to the physical world, discard those negative attitudes. Material things are composed of cosmic forces which originate in the wholeness of Consciousness.

Decline unsolicited mail or telephone financial investment propositions. Avoid participation in get-rich-quick schemes. Don't allow strangers or unqualified persons to manage your money or perform repairs on your home or property. When in doubt, obtain dependable professional advice from someone in your community who is well-known and respected.

The Flow of Money Conforms to the Same Natural Laws That Determine All of the Orderly Processes of Nature

When we are spiritually and mentally receptive to having money, and the channels through which money can flow to us are unobstructed, money is readily available. We make ourselves spiritually receptive by being aware of the wholeness of Consciousness in which everything we need already exists. We make ourselves mentally receptive by remembering that our mind is a part of the Cosmic Mind and by constructive, optimistic thinking. The channels through which money can flow to us remain open when we do what is necessary to allow ourselves to prosper. The great essential is to avoid thinking and behaving as though the wholeness of Consciousness could have limitations.

If you need more money, prepare to receive it by letting the universe know of your need. Instead of thinking that you will do something after you have money, visualize the ideal circumstances that you desire to experience as being already actualized. Needs can often be fulfilled without the use of money. So long as supportive events and circumstances unfold, you are prospering. If the satisfaction of your need or the actualization of your desire requires money, it will flow to you.

Real (authentic, genuine, sustained) prosperity cannot be experienced until awareness is clarified, thoughts are rational, emotions are regulated, and behaviors are constructive. All confining states of awareness and conflicted psychological conditions will have to be awakened from or outgrown. Ineffective behaviors will have to be replaced by behaviors which are life-enhancing. By diligent self-training in assuming and maintaining a prosperity consciousness and experiencing its results, that state of consciousness and circumstances which correspond to it will soon be normal for you.

Prepare a Personal Financial Statement

A personal financial statement is an itemized description of your physical assets and their current value, and your debts or financial obligations which must be paid. After subtracting the amount of money you owe to your creditors, the surplus is your net (remaining) financial worth. If you ever asked to borrow money from a bank or another money lending institution, you were probably asked to provide a personal financial statement. If you have never prepared a personal financial statement, or have not done so recently, to have an accurate assessment of the value of what you own, prepare one now. Doing this will help you to more realistically confront your current financial circumstances and enable you to plan your near and future actions. It will also prompt you to examine your thoughts, feelings, and behaviors concerning money, material things, and personal relationships.

First, write a list of your checking accounts, savings accounts, bank certificates of deposit, stocks, bonds, trust funds, annuities, and all other places where you have money deposited or invested. Include what you have in your pocket or purse. The total is the money you have.

Next, inventory the material things you own and their estimated value: a house or condominium; real estate; automobiles; furniture; clothing; books; machinery or tools; works of art that have value; leftover money from foreign travel that wasn't exchanged for your government's currency when you returned home; jewelry; gemstones; rare coins; precious metals—anything that could be converted to money.

Itemize your financial obligations. Subtract this amount from the value of your money and possessions to learn your current financial net worth. Finally, itemize the weekly, monthly, and annual costs to maintain your lifestyle or do the things you want to do. You will then have a clear mental picture and a written record of your financial situation.

You will probably discover that you have more assets than you thought you did. If you need money, you perhaps have things that could be sold to someone who would want them. When selling things to others, place a fair value on them when possible, rather than sell them at distress prices. Exchange the value that things represent for the value that money represents so you can use it for another purpose.

When preparing your financial statement, it will be helpful to also itemize weekly, monthly, and annual costs which are necessary to maintain your lifestyle or do the things you want to do. You will then have a written record and a clear mental picture of your financial situation.

If you have not yet learned to manage money, if your money supply is frequently inadequate for your needs because it seems to "slip through your fingers" or you "don't know where it went," prepare a budget. The purpose for doing this is not to confine your awareness or to limit your flow of resources; it is to help you to be more conscious of how you are using the value that money represents. On a sheet of paper or in your personal journal write how much money you earn or will have available for your use for each week and month of the year. Write how much money is needed for your savings and investment plan, food, utilities, gasoline, car payments, rent or mortgage, insurance, charitable giving, clothing, household items, and other necessities. Keep a written record of how much you pay for goods and services. Adhere to your budget. Exchange the value that money represents for the value of that for which you use it. When you have a surplus, you can choose to save and invest it or use it for things you want. Nurture your prosperity consciousness.

Avoid nonessential buying and waste. Excess consumption depletes your money supply and can damage the environment. In 1998 it was estimated that ten billion

Example of a Savings and Investment Program
$3500 invested each year, earning 7 percent interest, compounded annually.

Year	Savings	Interest	Total
1.	3500	245.00	3,745.00
2.	3500	507.15	7,752.15
3.	3500	787.65	12,039.80
4.	3500	1,087.79	16,627.59
5.	3500	1,408.93	21,536.51
6.	3500	1,752.56	26,789.07
7.	3500	2,120.24	32,409.31
8.	3500	2,513.65	38,422.96
9.	3500	2,934.61	44,857.57
10.	3500	3,385.03	51,742.60
11.	3500	3,866.98	59,109.58
12.	3500	4,382.67	66,992.25
13.	3500	4,934.46	75,426.71
14.	3500	5,524.87	84,451.58
15.	3500	6,156.61	94,108.19
16.	3500	6,832.57	104,440.76
17.	3500	7,555.85	115,496.61
18.	3500	8,329.76	127,326.38
19.	3500	9,157.85	139,984.22
20.	3500	10,043.90	153,528.12

Note that by the 11th year, the annual earned interest exceeds the annual amount invested in the program. At the end of 20 years, $70,000 is regularly saved and invested; the accumulated interest is $83,528. After 25 years the total would be $236,868. After 30 years, the total would be $353,756, of which $105,000 would have been saved and invested; the accumulated interest would total: $248,756.

tons of material, was consumed in America alone, 37 tons for each person for the manufacture and supply of goods and services. Consumption of metal, glass, wood, cement, and chemicals increased 18-fold since the beginning of the 20th century. Billions of tons of waste material are buried in the ground every year. Approximately 100,000 synthetic chemicals used in manufactured items are harmful to animals, humans, and the environment. It is only recently that recycling (conversion and reuse of materials for manufactured items) has been implemented. In regard to material things, ask, "How much do I really need." Have what you need, take care of what you have, recycle materials that can be reused, avoid buying what you do not need. Live comfortably. Simplify your life. You do not have to deplete your financial resources to keep the national and global economy thriving or to compete with others.

Regularly Save and Invest a Portion of Your Income

During the last decade of the 20th century, most working people in America saved less than five percent of their annual income, in contrast to workers in Japan and a few other countries who commonly saved as much as twenty-five percent. In the United States, the median income for working people was estimated to be $35,000. If only ten percent of that amount ($3500) was saved each year, and invested for twenty years, with earned interest of seven percent retained in the investment program, the combined savings and accumulated interest would total $153,528. In thirty years the total would be more than $300,000. If more money was saved and invested, the total amount would be much larger. After retirement, with no further investments made, the annual interest earned would provide financial security and personal freedom to creatively and productively enjoy one's remaining years on the planet and to bequest a substantial amount of money to one's heirs or for charitable purposes.

The easiest way to save $3500 a year is to put $292 each month or $68 a week in a savings account that earns interest, then invest the annual savings and interest at the end of the year. Many people spend more than this amount on nonessentials: impulsive buying at the grocery store, clothes they don't really need, extra meals at restaurants, overtipping at restaurants or for other services rendered, unnecessary household items, excessive use of electricity and water, lengthy telephone conversations, buying at retail instead of at a discount, travel costs that are too expensive, and in other ways.

There are many practical ways to save money:

• If you are employed, when you receive your paycheck, before you do anything else, save ten percent to invest. Put the amount of money you will need for your estimated weekly cash expenditures in your pocket or purse. Put the rest in your checking account to pay your bills or to use for other meaningful purposes.
• Before shopping at the supermarket or at department stores, to avoid making nonessential purchases, write a list of what you intend to buy before you go.
• When you need to replace your car, instead of buying a new, current model at the full retail price, consider buying a used car that is one or two years old, in good condi-

tion, with low mileage. Have it checked by your mechanic. You will avoid having to pay the extra several thousand dollars that a new car would have cost (and the interest on the loan if you had to borrow money for the purchase).

• For furniture, stoves, refrigerators, television sets, computers, lawn mowers, tools, and other items, consider perusing the classified ads in your community newspaper. Because of having to relocate or because of other life-changes, many people are willing to sell quality items for immediate cash.

• When buying a house, or any expensive item, avoid long-term financial obligations when possible. If you make mortgage payments for ten, twenty, or thirty years, you will actually be spending (wasting) many thousands of dollars in interest charges.

• Make your home energy-efficient. Get your heating system tuned up. Check the doors and windows to make sure they have a tight seal when closed. Use less hot water. Have the water heater adjusted to avoid excessive water temperature. Clean the light fixtures and use energy-efficient light bulbs.

• Credit cards are a convenience (and in some instances, a necessity, especially when traveling, renting a car or paying for hotel rooms). When possible, to avoid excessive interest charges, only use a credit card for purchases which you can pay for when the bill comes in the mail. In 1998 the average amount owed by credit card users nationwide was $4,000. It was estimated that the combined outstanding debt of all credit card users was two hundred billion dollars. Approximately 40 percent of people who use credit cards pay their balance in full every month.

Young adults starting to work at the minimum wage who make less money, can still save ten percent of their earnings, invest it regularly, and increase their savings and investments as their earnings increase. If you already have money saved, or have derived money from the sale of nonessential things or from an inheritance, you can begin an investment program with a substantial sum of money. Some investment programs will earn more than a seven percent annual interest rate.

When paying money to someone for something you need or want, think of the transaction as an investment rather than as an expenditure. To *spend* is to use up, to deplete, to deprive or take the force or value from something. When the value that money represents is used to obtain something of equivalent value, value is not decreased. You have not then actually spent (depleted or used up) the value; you still have it in another form. Value is only spent when a money transaction is made to obtain something of lesser value. When you pay money to obtain something that has more value than the money represents, the value you have is increased. While it may not always be possible to purchase something which has greater value than the money used for the transaction, at least endeavor to obtain an equivalent value.

Be a conscientious steward (manager) of money and other material resources while retaining your dignity and personal values. Be prudent (use good judgment) without becoming penurious (stingy or miserly). If money management is unfamiliar to you, when you need advice, obtain the best professional advice, and don't be shy about asking questions when details are unclear to you.

Money invested in well-managed companies that provide needed products and services can be good for long-term gains. From 1926 to 1999, average returns for such companies in the United States were 12.9 percent annually, with some annual returns lower and some higher. During the last decade of the 20th century, the value of some stocks increased at the rate of 25 percent or more annually. Unless you have surplus money and stock market investment knowledge and experience, it is best not to speculate, hoping that you will realize a quick and substantial return. Instead, stay with long-term investments in strong, well-managed companies. Even if the dividends are modest, through the years the value of your investment will steadily increase. If you do have surplus money to invest and are knowledgeable enough to choose stocks with growth potential, use only a portion of your funds for this purpose.

Avoid stock brokers who aggressively attempt to advise you to frequently sell your stock and buy another one, or who offer tempting opportunities that seem too good to be true. They earn a fee for each transaction. Make sure your stock broker or financial adviser is working for your benefit. Find one who charges a fair but modest fee for handling your transactions. Get the business terms in writing and examine them carefully before signing any documents or making investments.

Your financial adviser or a bank officer should be able to inform you about other prudent ways to invest for a fair rate of return, such as in bonds or in a secure, well-managed fund which provides an annuity. Some bonds issued by municipalities may earn lower interest which is tax-free. An annuity is an annual, predetermined or fixed payment of income from an investment program for a lifetime or a specified number of years.

Decide on your life-choices before choosing an investment program. Determine your needs or wishes, then
invest so that your flow of money will be more than
adequate to enable you to accomplish your purposes.
Before starting a long-term investment program, put the
equivalent of three to six months of living expenses in a
savings account or short-term bank certificate of deposit
to have available if you need it. Pay any outstanding debts.
Unpaid debts will damage your credit rating. Debts paid
over a period of time often require high interest payments.

If you have initiative and are innovative, there are
other ways to earn money. An investment in real estate
or in properties that can be rented or leased can be profit-
able. If investing in undeveloped real estate which is
certain to increase in value, management skills can be
minimal. You will only have to make arrangements to
obtain the site and pay the annual property tax. For real
estate with buildings on it, insurance premiums will have
to be paid. Before making a purchase, have your attorney
do the necessary research to verify that the site has no
outstanding liens against it for back taxes or other financial obligations, that the boundaries are clearly defined,
and that the zoning laws are suitable for your purposes.
Properties which are rented or leased will require more
attention to details. Most communities have professional
management companies which will write the contracts
and collect the rent or lease payments for a modest fee.
Have your attorney examine and approve all legal documents. Before retaining an attorney, find out ahead of time
what the costs will be for the legal services you require.

Invest money only in material things which will

increase in value. Real estate, in areas where the population is growing rapidly, usually increases in value through
the years. Metals, such as silver, gold, and platinum, which
are considered to be precious (of high value) because of
their rarity and durability, are only good investments if
purchased at a low price. Most coins made of such metals
which may be advertised as being good investments, are
not—their worth is that of the metal which can be melted
and reused. Gemstones—diamonds, rubies, sapphires, and
a few others which have been used for centuries to represent value—are good for investment purposes only if they
are of excellent quality and obtained at low (wholesale or
below) prices. The value attributed to gemstones (and to
all material things) is arbitrary, determined by individual
judgment rather than stable or real. Antique furniture,
art, and other items commonly referred to as collectibles,
represent value only if someone is willing to pay more
than your cost to acquire them.

Learning to manage money and other resources can
be a helpful spiritual exercise that will provide insight
into how your actions produce effects and motivate you to
be responsible for your behaviors. You will be challenged
to think rationally, effectively use your powers of intelligence and intuition, and cultivate patience. As your awareness expands, you will discover that all aspects of life are
inseparably interrelated.

Conscious Giving is Always Beneficial;
Tithing May Not Always Be Beneficial

The most helpful contribution you can make to others
and the planet is to actualize your prosperity conscious-

ness by unfolding and expressing your spiritual qualities and living wholesomely and effectively. Your Self-realization and constructive actions will then be nurturing and supportive. Everyone with whom you relate on a personal basis, as well as the collective consciousness of all life, will be benefited. It can also be helpful to reach out in practical ways by seeing needs and filling them and seeing hurts and doing what you can to heal them.

Whatever you do to be helpful, do consciously. Understand what is needed and provide it in the most useful way possible. Be as clear-minded in your giving as you are in making decisions and performing actions for the well-being of yourself, your family, and members of your community.

You may be able to be helpful by volunteering your knowledge and skills to individuals in need of help and to organized endeavors which provide social, economic, medical, cultural, environmental, and spiritual services. You can also give money to organizations which you know to be providing services which are of value. When you do, find out if they are well-managed and if the money you give will be used for the purposes for which you give it. Don't give because of sentiment; give with conscious intention, with charity (Latin, *caritas*, affection, love).

Some groups which are organized for religious purposes encourage their members to tithe (give ten percent of their income) regularly. Members who derive benefit from the programs and services provided by the organization or approve of the educational and charitable work that is freely offered, should provide financial support in accord with their means. Financial appeals made by representatives of the organization should not be coercive (threatening or intimidating). Anyone who asserts that ten percent of your income is "God's money" or that it is your "duty" to give that much is irrational. Make your own wise choices. Giving should be regulated by your ability to give and your sense of appropriateness.

References to tithing in the Old Testament are related to the period of time in the Middle East when Levitical law demanded a tithe as a form of taxation required of members of Hebrew communities. Ten percent of one's income or possessions was taxed to provide funds for the government which provided services for the people. It was not a voluntary or charitable contribution, just as the federal, state, county, personal property or sales taxes we pay today are not voluntary or charitable contributions.

Some members of religious organizations are told that when they tithe to the organization, they will be blessed and prospered. If most of the members of a large congregation tithed on a regular schedule, the organization would surely prosper; all who tithed might not prosper. To prosper, our awareness has to be clarified and receptive to flows of good fortune. If our awareness is not clear, if our mental and emotional states are conflicted, if we give with the hope that God or the universe will give us something in return, giving may benefit those to whom we give but will not benefit us.

The spiritually aware, healthy-minded way to give money to a worthwhile cause is to give freely in accord with your ability because you know, and feel at the innermost level of your Being, that it is the right thing to do, without any need for personal recognition or reward. You are then a conduit through which benefits flow. Giving in this way keeps your awareness clear and your relationships with life well-ordered.

Regular, conscious, thoughtful, useful giving for worthwhile purposes is a helpful money-management discipline. It will be of benefit to others. It will remind you of the importance of being a prudent caretaker of the value that money represents. It will allow you to creatively interact with the universe in which you live.

Plan For the Orderly Distribution
of Your Wealth When You Will No
Longer Need It

Regardless of your calendar age, if you have money or material things, itemize them and have your attorney prepare a will, a legal document in which your wishes for having your money and possessions distributed are clearly defined. From time to time, as your wealth increases or as circumstances change, a codicil (a supplement or appendix) can be added. Put your will in a safe place and let your attorney and one or two responsible family members or close friends know where it is.

In your will, make provisions for paying any outstanding financial obligations and specifically describe how the remainder of your estate is to be distributed. In the absence of a will, an officer of the court may be assigned the duty of disposing of your estate. Just as you are now attentive to managing your money and other resources in a caring and thoughtful manner, prepare written instructions for having your wealth constructively used after you leave this world.

If you have abundant resources, retain what you will need for the remainder of your physical life and distribute the surplus to your heirs and to charitable causes before you go. You will have the satisfaction of knowing that your wealth is being used constructively and its value will immediately be helpful to others. To delay the use of excess wealth for meaningful purposes is to deny others the benefits they could have or might need. Clinging to excess money—whether thousands, millions, or billions of dollars—or to material things which are no longer needed, is detrimental to psychological health and interferes with spiritual growth. Strong attachments of any kind are symptoms of self-centeredness and insecurity which, when outgrown, allow the unfoldment of innate soul qualities to more easily occur.

Live wisely, appropriately, and effectively so that when you leave this world no duties are uncompleted and your awareness is clear. You will then be able to easily withdraw your attention from the mundane realm and fully awaken to higher realities.

While improving your knowledge and functional skills and using both to the fullest extent possible, be ever conscious of the all-pervasive, benevolent Reality with purposes you are to serve and which provides for your needs. As you become more spiritually awake, you will perceive it as being both impersonal and personal—as larger, yet not other, than you—as *that* in which everything exists and by which everything is nurtured.

Whatever is true, honest, just, pure, pleasing, and is known to be of value; if it has virtue and provides cause to be thankful, think on these things.

– New Testament / *Philippians* 4.8
Modern translation

CHAPTER EIGHT

Established in Prosperity Consciousness, Fulfill Your Destiny

It is every soul's destiny—the inevitable culmination of its lengthy and sometimes burdensome sojourn in space and time—to be spiritually enlightened. Having fully awakened from its former semiconscious "dream" of limitations and mortality, its powers of perception unfettered, with nothing more to be accomplished, its serene bliss ever-new, it enjoys endless freedom.

How rapidly this final illumination of consciousness emerges is determined by the soul's capacity to intellectually and intuitively perceive the reality of the wholeness of life and comprehend its processes. As long as the soul's awareness is unconsciously identified with conditioned mental and physical states, it will be confined and restricted by them. When its awareness is consciously removed from debilitating involvements with conditioned mental states, it is restored to its innate purity.

Incidents of temporary enlightenment may occur spontaneously, allowing fleeting glimpses of higher realities which are not ordinarily perceived. Partial enlightenment can also result from intellectual inquiry, prayerful contemplation, and meditation practice to the stage of alert, thought-free awareness independent of sensory perceptions, thoughts, or emotional states. By frequent evocation (bringing forth rather than trying to cause or create) of superconscious states, transcendent perceptions become more frequent, proficiency in mastering states of consciousness is acquired, and Self-realization persists.

For some truth seekers, the gap between the stage where they feel themselves to be in their spiritual growth and where they aspire to be, seems vast. They may ask, "How can I possibly get there from where I am?" Thankfully, the presumed distance between states of awareness is an illusion, a faulty perception.

Awakening through the stages of spiritual growth is an inner, soul-directed process; it is not determined by time or external conditions. The only obstacles to overcome are the subconscious conditionings one has accumulated, egocentric preoccupation with habitual ways of thinking and behavior, and a deficiency of sincere desire to be spiritually awake and freely functional. Subconscious conditionings (karmic or causative influences) can be weakened, eliminated, and their forces transformed to be used for higher purposes. Habits of thinking and behavior can be changed. Sincere desire to be spiritually awake can be nurtured by making right choices and performing constructive actions.

Enlightenment is the result of awakening to the facts of life rather than an effect produced by a mundane cause. The intentional actions we perform to harmoniously integrate the spiritual, mental, physical, and environmental components of our lives are therapeutic (healing); they remove inner and outer conditions which restrict our endeavors to perceive with accuracy and function effectively.

The most healing action we can immediately perform is to rid ourselves of mental attitudes and feelings which reinforce self-centeredness, confine awareness, impair intellectual powers, perpetuate psychological conflicts, prevent the establishment and maintenance of cooperative personal relationships, and restrict spiritual growth. The mental attitudes and feelings to be renounced are: hatred; shame, fear; grief; condemnation of self or others; racial, ethnic, cultural, or religious prejudice; extravagant pride in regard to one's ancestry or to social or financial status; and arrogance (smug self-righteousness). To cling to or nurture any of these characteristics is to wantonly engage in self-defeating behaviors.

Our degree of spiritual awareness, (and the understanding which corresponds to it) is always being confirmed by the thoughts we habitually think, the feelings we allow to prevail, the actions we perform, the relationships we nurture, and the circumstances which we choose, attract, or allow to manifest and persist. The life-enhancing incidents which occur and the supportive material circumstances which result from our sustained prosperity consciousness are by-products. Their value is the physical security and comfort they provide that allows us the freedom to explore higher realms of mind and spirit and to express our creative abilities without being unduly burdened by concerns regarding mundane matters.

If you cannot always assume a soul- and God-centered state of awareness at will because of the disruptive influences of restless thoughts or impelling moods, use your intellectual and intuitive powers to discern your relationship to the wholeness of Consciousness. Behind the currents of thoughts that flow through your mind and the emotional surges that rise and decline, acknowledge the ever-shining reality of pure consciousness and identify your awareness with it.

The infinite ocean of Consciousness is the Source and essence of everything. Remain anchored in the Source. Serve the Source. Give of yourself to the Source. Receive from the Source. Relate to the world with understanding. Live in the world without attachments to it or its varied manifestations. The more spiritually aware you are, the more easily you will be able to relate to space, time, events, and circumstances.

Whenever you have difficulty in solving everyday problems, confronting and overcoming obstacles, or relating to others, scan your memories with dispassionate objectivity. Be patient when a duration of time is required for favorable events to transpire. Anchor your awareness in the Source—which is identical with your innermost level of Being. When you are serenely poised, your prosperity consciousness will provide for all of your needs and make possible the rapid fulfillment of your spiritual destiny.

Glossary

Words are symbols used to define and communicate ideas and concepts. It will be helpful to know the meanings of these words. If necessary, refer to a dictionary to learn the precise definitions of other words used in the text.

affirmation A declaration of truth or fact.

affluence A flowing toward, a plentiful supply.

aspiration To "rise upward." To hope or fervently desire.

attentive Observant, focused, concentrated.

aware Conscious, alert, perceptive.

being The quality or state of existing.

Being When spelled with an upper case *B* the word is used to refer to one's essence or true nature: pure consciousness.

choose To select from several possible alternatives.

clear Unobstructed or pure.

concentration An unwavering flow of attention.

consciousness 1. The state of being aware. 2. The totality of knowledge, opinions, attitudes, and beliefs of an individual or group.

Consciousness When spelled with an upper case *C*, the word is used to refer to the one self-existent reality (God).

decisive Conclusive. Without doubt. Determined.

delusion Any erroneous belief or opinion. The belief that one is a mortal, mind-body creature rather than an immortal, spiritual being is a commonly accepted delusion and the primary cause of all other delusions that contribute to the misfortune and suffering of human beings.

effective Having a desired or intended effect. Effective living results in the accomplishment of intended purposes.

essence The indispensable, inner element or quality.

grace Latin *gratia*, good will; from *gratus*, pleasing. Divine care and provision bestowed freely. Life-enhancing impulses from within the field of omnipresent Consciousness and from within the soul (individualized Being) cause supportive actions and events to occur. The actions of grace and their effects can be received. They cannot be caused to occur.

happy Characterized by satisfaction, joy, pleasure.

health A condition of optimal (most favorable) well-being.

healthy-minded The mental condition characterized by cheerfulness, contentment, optimism, rational thinking, and psychological health.

illumination Intellectual and spiritual enlightenment. One's consciousness is illumined when the faculty of intellect is purified and awareness is no longer fragmented or clouded.

illusion A misperception. Illusions have objects (concepts, things, events, sensations, or circumstances) which are inaccurately perceived. The universe is not an illusion; our misperceptions of the universe are illusions.

imagination The ability to form a mental picture or concept of something which is not present or does not yet exist. An act of *creative* imagination differs from fantasy in that it is intentionally produced and consciously controlled by concentrated attention.

intellect Latin *intellectus*, perception. The mental faculty that enables one to discriminate, discern, comprehend, and think rationally.

life 1. Manifested in functions such as growth, metabolism, response to stimuli, and reproduction. 2. The interval of experiences that constitute one's existence. 3. The spiritual state which transcends space and time.

mantra From the Sanskrit verb-root *man*, to think. When a meditator's attention is focused on a word, word-phrase, or sound (mantra), it withdraws from physical sensations and mental processes and "goes beyond" them.

meaningful Having value, especially functional value. To live with conscious intention and experience the fulfillment of all of life's purposes is to live meaningfully.

meditation Contemplative concentration on a chosen object (focus of attention) or ideal. Attentive meditation practice reduces stress, calms and pacifies the mind and emotions, clarifies awareness, and elicits superconscious states.

mind Sanskrit *manas*, thinking faculty. The mind processes information. Its physical organ is the brain. There is one Cosmic Mind of which all individualized minds are units.

mind-body constitution The basic psychological and physiological characteristics of living things. When they are balanced and coordinated, health and functional abilities are at their most favorable levels.*

money A commodity (something considered to be of value) used to conveniently pay for things or services considered to be of equivalent value. Word origin: Latin *Moneta*, an epithet (descriptive substitute name) for *Juno*, a mythical goddess whose temple in ancient Rome housed the mint where the country's metal coins were manufactured.

participate To take part in, to be attentively involved with an activity, relationship, or process.

possibility That which is capable of existing, happening, or being true without contradicting natural laws, facts, or circumstances.

possibility-thinking Thinking about and clearly visualizing favorable possibilities.

primordial nature *Primordial*: occurring first in a sequence of events. *Nature*: the essential properties of the mundane world, the expressive energies of Consciousness, cosmic forces, space, and time.

prosper To thrive, to flourish, to be fulfilled. Prosperity is actualized and experienced when the spiritual, physical, mental, and environmental components of one's life are harmoniously integrated.

purpose A desired or intended result or effect.

---

* For a better understanding of the mind-body constitution and supportive lifestyle regimens, refer to the author's book *An Easy Guide to Ayurveda*.

rational Reasonable. Rational thinking is practical and well-ordered because supported by intelligence and knowledge.

realization Complete comprehension of something.

resolve An unwavering intention or sincere commitment to do something.

result The consequence, outcome, or effect of an intention, thought, word, or physical action.

self-conscious The state during which one's awareness is identified with the illusional sense of selfhood (ego) and personality characteristics.

Self-realization The true Self is the essence of one's Being. When this is experienced and known, one is Self-realized.

serene Peaceful, tranquil.

spiritual Of or related to God or to the soul.

subliminal Below the threshold of conscious perception.

superconscious Awareness unmodified by subconscious and ordinary waking states and their influences.

technique A systematic procedure used to accomplish a purpose. The technique of creative imagination can be used to adjust states of awareness and visualize possibilities. A meditation technique (such as prayer, contemplation of a mantra, or breath awareness) can be used to elicit physical relaxation, calm mental activities and pacify the emotions, and improve concentration.

whole Complete, undivided. The universe is whole. Its forces, energies, attributes, and manifestations are its aspects. The

soul's awareness is experienced as being whole when the
mental and emotional conditions which blur and distort it
are pacified or removed.

will 1. *Core meaning*: unrestricted freedom to choose. 2. The
ability to make decisions and act independently. 3. A legal
written description of one's wishes for the distribution of
financial assets and personal possessions.

willing Eager to act or respond gladly.

yoga Sanskrit, "to bring together" or unify one's awareness
with the infinite Consciousness. Yoga practices pacify and
remove mental and emotional restrictions that confine the
practitioner's awareness. The procedures used should be suitable for the practitioner as determined by psychological tem-
perament and capacity for practice and experience. Hatha
yoga, with emphasis on physical routines, has become popular in recent years. Its real purpose is to nurture total health
and culminate in mastery of the senses and mental processes
so that one can live effectively and become proficient in meditation practice.

Roy Eugene Davis is an internationally traveled teacher of spiritual growth processes with emphasis on purposeful living and proficiency in meditation practice. The founder-director of Center for Spiritual Awareness, he has presented lectures and seminars in more than one hundred North American cities, Japan, Europe, Brazil, India, and West Africa. Some of his many books have been published in ten languages. Mr. Davis was ordained by Paramahansa Yogananda, (1951, Los Angeles California).

The meditation retreat center and administrative offices of Center for Spiritual Awareness are located on a secluded eleven acre site in the northeast Georgia mountains, near the North and South Carolina borders, ninety miles from Atlanta. Meditation retreats are offered on a regular schedule. CSA Press is the publishing and literature outreach department. A free information packet may be requested.

Center for Spiritual Awareness
Post Office Box 7 • Lakemont, Georgia 30552-0007
(706) 782-4723 Fax (706) 782-4560 e-mail csainc@stc.net
Internet Web Site www.csa-davis.org

On Lake Rabun Road, Lakemont, Georgia